W9-CNL-937

The Humorous Mr. Lincoln

The Humorous
Mr. Lincoln

KEITH W. JENNISON

BONANZA BOOKS · *New York*

Designed by Laurel Wagner

Manufactured in the United States of America

Library of Congress Catalog Card No. 65-26436

This edition published by Bonanza Books,
a division of Crown Publishers, Inc.
by arrangement with Thomas Y. Crowell Company

j k l m n o p

To Carl Sandburg, who wrote the Lincoln symphony, in love and gratitude for what he has given me in his books and of himself.

Foreword

The temptation to treat Abraham Lincoln as a god has not always been resisted by even his most distinguished biographers. Although this book will add little to most readers' knowledge of Mr. Lincoln's life, it is my hope that the particular arrangement of materials may create a fresh sense of companionship with the towering, and somewhat remote, figure of the sixteenth President of the United States.

My plan in writing the book was to set down, more or less in chronological order, all the best examples of Mr. Lincoln's humor with just enough narrative and scene-setting to give a sense of perspective. There being a confusion of final authorities as to the precise text of the anecdotes, I have chosen simply the versions that pleased me the most and for which there appeared to be *enough* authority.

Perhaps the only general remark that might be useful concerns the way Mr. Lincoln's use of humor changed. During the wilderness years he told jokes and stories without trying to prove anything at all; he told them simply because it was natural for him to do so. After he became a lawyer he found that his wit and his acute sense of the ridiculous were effective courtroom tools. As a politician he handled the weapon of satire as a stiletto or a broadax as the occasion demanded. During the first few months of his Presidency he used humor many times as a roundabout way of saying "no." As his responsibility grew and became almost unendurable he took to telling jokes again, trying to lessen the tensions in himself and those around him.

David R. Locke, an Ohio newspaperman who signed himself Petroleum V. Nasby, made this comment on Mr. Lincoln: "His flow of humor was a sparkling spring gushing out of a rock—the flashing water had a somber background which made it all the brighter."

Being in complete agreement with this opinion, I have tried to illustrate it by using both the humor itself and some of the darker background that makes the humor seem so bright. Regardless of the book's merits, or lack of them, I am confident that it will occupy the position that Mr. Lincoln himself predicted for a volume he was asked to criticize. "For those who like this kind of a book," he wrote, "this is the kind of book they will like."

K.W.J.

Acknowledgments

Emanuel Hertz dedicated his *Lincoln Talks* to: "All the speakers and writers who have ever used, or intend to use, a 'Lincoln story.'" I hereby cheerfully acknowledge my debt to Mr. Hertz's fine book which is, perhaps, the most complete collection of Lincoln anecdotes. Special thanks are due to the staff of the John Hay Library of Brown University for giving me access to the McClellan Lincoln Collection. I am deeply indebted to James N. Adams of the Illinois State Historical Library for reading the manuscript and making invaluable suggestions and corrections. I am further indebted to the Illinois State Historical Library for permission to reprint its Lincoln Chronology, edited by the late Harry Pratt.

To Huddee Herrick of Marlboro College who understood exactly what kind of material I was looking for and helped me mightily, and to my wife Emily who did far more than correct the typescript, I offer a grateful heart.

K.W.J.

Illustrations

The Humorous Mr. Lincoln

[1]

The Kentucky boy with the coarse black hair and gray eyes learned early that the only way to fight a wilderness was to cultivate it. He knew how to clear land, plow it, plant it, hoe it, and weed it before he knew how to spell.

He found out that sometimes you get a good crop, sometimes you get a poor crop, and sometimes you don't get any crop at all. About all you could do was work and hope; maybe the wolves wouldn't kill so many sheep next year; maybe flood and frost would spare the corn; maybe the birds and bears wouldn't eat all the berries and other fruit; and maybe the skunks would leave the chickens alone—but you never knew for sure.

Still, Tom Lincoln and his son were better off than half the laborers of Hardin County. If you were free and white, what you raised belonged to you; if you were slave and black, it didn't.

During the seven years that the boy lived in Kentucky he had some schooling. He learned how to spell his name and that, in arithmetic, two and two always added up to four.

There wasn't much humor in the wilderness except what a man could put there, and Tom Lincoln, who was good with a yarn, did the best he knew how. Later on, Abe said, "My father taught me how to work, but not to love it. I never did like work and I admit it. I'd rather read, tell stories, crack jokes, talk, laugh—anything but work."

In regard to his ancestry, Abe said, "I don't know who my grandfather was. I am much more concerned to know what his grandson will be."

1

Lincoln's famous birthplace, a log cabin in Kentucky, has become a symbol for the American dream—the ability to rise to the top from the most humble beginnings. Abe claimed he didn't know who his grandfather was, and was much more concerned about what his grandson would be.

Tom Lincoln had some trouble about the ownership of the land he was paying taxes on in Kentucky and decided to move along to Indiana, once the farm could be sold. Meanwhile he kept right on working the Kentucky farm, because as he said, "Every man must skin his own skunk." When a neighbor asked him why he was taking such good care of the place when he had to sell it, Tom answered, "So I do, but I ain't going to let my farm find it out."

In 1816 the Lincolns moved to Indiana, and Abe helped his father build a cabin on Little Pigeon Creek in Buckhorn Valley.

Many years later he wrote: "We settled in an unbroken forest, and the clearing away of surplus wood was the great task ahead. I, though very young, was very large for my age, and had an ax put in my hands at once; and from that till within my twenty-third year I was almost constantly handling that most useful instrument—less, of course, in plowing and harvest seasons.

"Our new home was in a wild region with many bears and other wild animals still in the woods. There I took my early start as a hunter, which was never much improved afterward. A few days before the completion of my eighth year, in the absence of my father, a flock of wild turkeys approached the new log cabin, and I with a rifle-gun, standing inside, shot through a crack and killed one of them. I have never since pulled a trigger on any larger game.

"It was pretty pinching at times at first in Indiana, getting the cabin built, and clearing for the crops, but presently we got reasonably comfortable."

Abe lived there with his father and mother and sister Sally for a little over a year. At night in the cabin his mother, the sensitive and lonely Nancy Hanks, would sing what she remembered of the great English ballads that she had learned as a child in Virginia, and read aloud to the children from the Bible, *Aesop's Fables*, and *The Pilgrim's Progress*. In

3

1818 Abe's mother died, and after a decent interval Tom brought home the widow Sally Bush Johnston as his wife, and Abe and Sally's stepmother. She was a warm and loving woman, and Abe cherished her all his life.

Occasionally the new family group included Abe's cousin Dennis Hanks, and once when Abe was reading *Aesop's Fables* aloud, Dennis said:

"Abe, them yarns is all lies."

Abe didn't even look up from his reading. "Mighty darn good lies, Denny," he said.

He was beginning to be fascinated by language. "Among my earliest recollections I remember how, when a mere child, I used to get irritated when anybody talked to me in a way I could not understand. I can remember going into my little bedroom, after hearing the neighbors talk of an evening with my father, and spending no small part of the night trying to make out what was the exact meaning of some of their, to me, dark sayings. I could not sleep, although I tried to, when I got on such a hunt for an idea, until I had caught it; and when I thought I had got it I was never satisfied until I had repeated it over and over again, until I had put it in language plain enough, as I thought, for any boy I knew to comprehend."

Here in Indiana the boy finished a few more months of schooling. Abe and Sally walked eighteen miles a day to get what little instruction they got. One of his school books was a book of sums that he wrote out and bound himself. On one page the following lines appear:

Abraham Lincoln
his hand and pen
he will be good but
god knows When.

Later on, he told a story about this school. "All our reading was done from the Bible and we stood up in a long line

4

and read the scriptures aloud. One day our lesson was about the faithful Israelites who were thrown into the fiery furnace and were delivered by the Lord without so much as being scorched. One little fellow had to read the verses in which appeared, for the first time, the names of Shadrach, Meshach and Abednego. The boy stumbled on Shadrach, floundered on Meshach and went all to pieces on Abednego. Instantly the hand of the teacher gave him a cuff on the head that left him wailing and blubbering as the next boy in line went on with the reading. By the time the first round was over he had quieted down and stopped sniffling.

"His blunder and disgrace were forgotten by the others in the class until it was almost his turn to read again. Suddenly he sent up a wail which alarmed even the teacher, who with rather unusual gentleness asked, 'What's the matter now?'

"Pointing with a shaking finger at the verse which in a few minutes would fall to him to read, the boy managed to stammer, 'Look there, teacher, there comes those same damn three fellows again.' "

Abe had less than a year of total attendance at school. But he discovered books. It was said that there wasn't a book within fifty miles of the Lincoln cabin that he hadn't read, and in his own words, "The things I want to know are in books. My best friend is the man who'll get me a book I ain't read."

Many years later, in the White House, he commented on his appetite for books, and an ambitious guest commented that men of force could get along without them by doing their own thinking instead of adopting what other men thought. Lincoln brought him up short by saying: "Books serve to show a man that those original thoughts of his aren't very new after all."

Abe read the Bible all his life; the epics, the melodramas, the tales of heroes and villains, the songs, the poetry, and the lamentations. The great somber reflections of the book Ecclesiastes: "To every thing there is a season, and a time to

5

every purpose under the heaven," stayed with him all his life.

Going to church was sometimes a different thing entirely, according to a story Abe told the first day he spent in New Salem.

"A preacher back in Indiana was delivering a sermon in a log meeting house in the woods. The preacher was wearing old-fashioned baggy pantaloons fastened with one button and no suspenders. His shirt was fastened at the neck with one button. In a loud voice the preacher announced his text for the day. 'I am the Christ whom I shall represent this day.' About that time a little blue lizard ran up one leg of the pantaloons. The preacher went ahead with his sermon, slapping at his legs. After awhile the lizard came so high the preacher got desperate, and, going on with his sermon, unbuttoned his pants, let them fall down and kicked them off. By this time the lizard had changed his route and was circling around under his shirt. The preacher, repeating his text, 'I am the Christ whom I shall represent today,' loosened his shirt button and off came the shirt. The congregation sat in the pews dazed and dazzled. Everything was still for a minute, then a dignified elderly lady stood up, pointed a finger at the pulpit and called out at the top of her voice: 'I just want to say, sir, that if you represent Jesus Christ, then I'm done with the Bible.' "

One traveling preacher who was visiting a frontier family lectured them on their apparent godlessness. There was no Bible immediately apparent in their cabin, although the mother claimed that they did own one. The children were dispatched to find it. Finally a few tattered pages were brought to light.

"I had no idea," the mother said, "that we were so nearly out."

Another story Lincoln told concerned a southern Illinois preacher who asserted that the Saviour was the only perfect man who had ever appeared in this world; also, that there was no record in the Bible, or any place else, of a perfect woman having lived. The preacher was interrupted by a lady in the congregation who rose to her feet and said:

"I know a perfect woman, and I've heard about her every day for the last six years."

"Who was she?" the minister asked.

"My husband's first wife," the lady answered.

Lincoln didn't like prepared sermons. He said he liked to have the preacher act as if he were fighting a swarm of bees.

[2]

Maybe Abe didn't like to work, but now that he was full grown and strong as a young bull he didn't do much else. He worked for his father and helped out the neighbors. Still, he found time to read everything he could lay his hands on, and practiced penmanship till he got so he was writing letters for everybody in the community who could not write his own.

He had acquired Weems's *Life of Washington,* a life of Ben Franklin, and the text of a document he was to have intimate dealings with—the Constitution of the United States. He wrestled and ran, and read and wrote, and practiced giving speeches to trees.

The year Abe was twenty-one his father was ready to move again; this time to Illinois. Abe had saved thirty-six dollars and invested them in a peddler's stock of needles, pins, and notions. The family was traveling by oxcart, and he had time to offer his wares to the widely separated cabins along the way. One visit he made gave him the basis for a story he later used most effectively:

Always a voracious reader, Lincoln began studying law when he found a copy of Blackstone's *Commentaries* in the bottom of a barrel. In 1844 he and a partner, William H. Herndon, opened the above office in Springfield.

"Just before we left Indiana and crossed into Illinois we came across a small farmhouse full of children. These ranged in years from seventeen years to seventeen months, and all were in tears. The mother of the family was red-headed and red-faced, and the whip she held in her right hand led to the inference that she had just been chastising her brood. The father of the family, a meek-looking, mild-mannered, tow-headed chap, was standing in the front doorway, awaiting, to all appearances, his turn to feel the thong.

"I thought there wasn't much use in asking the head of that house whether she wanted any notions. She was too busy. It was evident that an insurrection had been in progress, but it was pretty well quelled when I got there. The mother had about suppressed it with an iron hand, but she was not running any risks. She kept a stern and wary eye on all the children, not forgetting an occasional glance at 'the old man' in the doorway.

"She saw me as I came up, and from her look I was of the opinion that she thought I was about to interfere. Advancing to the doorway and roughly pushing her husband aside, she demanded to know my business.

" 'Nothing, Madam,' I answered as gently as possible; 'I merely dropped in as I came along to see how things were going.

" 'Well, you needn't wait,' she said, 'there's trouble here and lots of it, but I can manage my own affairs without the help of outsiders. This is just a family row, but I'll teach these brats their places if I have to lick the hide off every one of them. I don't do much talking but I run this house, and don't want no one sneaking around trying to find out how I do it!' "

President Lincoln told this story during a Cabinet meeting which was considering the interest that many foreign powers were taking in the War between the States.

"That's the case here with us," the President went on, "we

9

must let other nations know that we propose to settle our family row in our own way and teach these brats their places if we have to lick the hide off of each and every one of them. And like that old woman, we don't want any sneaking around by other countries who would like to find out how we are going to do it, either.

"Now, Seward, you write some diplomatic notes to that effect."

[3]

In his twenty-third year Abe left home for good and went out on his own. He helped build a flatboat and traveled down to New Orleans where he saw human beings bought and sold like cattle. Upon his return he settled in New Salem, working at odd jobs, cutting and splitting walnut fence rails to earn money for food and clothes. He helped out at store-keeping and quickly established the reputation for being "the cleverest fellow who ever broke into the settlement," a comment made by Jack Armstrong, the local strong-boy, after picking himself up off the ground where Abe had flung him.

Abe had a way of saying things that were laughed at, delighted in, and remembered. One evening in a crowd that had gathered outside Offutt's store a man was boasting about his horse galloping nine miles without drawing a long breath. After repeating the boast several times he asked Abe what he thought about the performance.

"Well, Uncle," Abe said, "now tell us how many short breaths he drew."

During this time the label "Honest Abe" was fastened on

the young man to stay. Once or twice he made a mistake of a few pennies in giving change; or of using a wrong weight on the scale and sending a customer away with a fraction less than had been paid for. On these occasions Abe closed up the store and sought out the customer to rectify the error.

These were also the days when a steamboat attempted to run on the Sangamon River. The ship was referred to as the "Try-weekly Steamer—goes up one week and tries to come down the next." Abe worked aboard the craft for a while, but as the average speed was four miles a day he didn't think he was getting anywhere very fast.

In the spring of 1832, "encouraged by his great popularity among his immediate neighbors," he announced himself as a candidate for the General Assembly of the State. The hand-bill which he wrote to announce his candidacy ended with this paragraph:

"Every man is said to have his peculiar ambition. Whether it is true or not, I cannot say. I can only speak for one man. I have no thought so great as that of being esteemed of my fellow men by rendering myself worthy of their esteem. How far I shall succeed in gratifying this ambition is yet to be developed. I was born and have remained in the most humble walks of life. I have no wealthy or popular relations or friends to recommend me. My case is thrown exclusively on the independent voters of the county; and, if elected, they will have conferred a favor upon me for which I shall be unremitting in my labors to compensate. But if the good people in their wisdom shall see fit to keep me in the background, I have been too familiar with disappointments to be very much chagrined."

One of his early speeches in the campaign was made in Pappsville to a group that had assembled for an auction. Before he could start speaking, a fight started, in which one of his friends was about to "succumb to the attack of an infurated ruffian." Lincoln stepped down from the platform and tossed the offender, as one witness claimed, "twelve feet away." He then mounted the platform and gave the following address:

"Fellow citizens, I presume you all know who I am. I am humble Abraham Lincoln. I have been solicited by many to become a candidate for the legislature. My politics are short and sweet—like the old woman's dance. I am in favor of a national bank. I am in favor of the internal improvement system, and a high protective tariff. These are my sentiments and political principles. If elected, I shall be thankful; if not it will be all the same."

It was this same spring of 1832 that old Chief Black Hawk led his braves back into the lands that he had sold, and again white men and red men practiced atrocities on each other in the wilderness.

The regular army detachments sent out to subdue Black Hawk were augmented by volunteer regiments. Abe was urged to form a volunteer company and, as he figured it wouldn't do his campaign any harm, agreed to do so. Captain Lincoln's company was officially designated as "mounted," but neither the captain nor the troops had any horses. In response to the first direct military order he issued he was told to go to hell. He didn't have much better luck on the parade ground. One day the young captain was marching his two platoons toward a narrow gate and couldn't recall what the order was to pass them through the gate two by two. He settled this problem by commanding:

"This company is dismissed for two minutes. It will fall in on the other side of the gate."

As a matter of record, Lincoln's men were rough and unmanageable to the point that their captain was court-martialed for not being able to control them. The court ordered Captain Lincoln to carry a wooden sword for two days.

The young captain was conscious of his extraordinary height and customarily walked with a slouch. His colonel was a miniature martinet of five feet. The colonel braced Abe one day and made him stand as straight and tall as he could.

"Am I always to remain so?" Abe asked.

"Certainly, fellow," the colonel replied.

"Then goodbye, Colonel," Abe said, "for I shall never see you again."

One night part of the company had a brief skirmish with the enemy, and when they were reassembled in camp it was discovered that Lincoln was missing.

"Captain Abe," one of the men said, when Lincoln approached the camp, "is that you? Thought you were killed."

"Yes," Lincoln said, "this is me. Ain't killed either."

"Didn't run away, did you?"

"No," the captain answered, "I don't think I ran away. But, after all, I reckon if anybody had seen me going, and had been told I was going for a doctor, he would have thought somebody was almighty sick."

The only encounter Captain Lincoln had with a live Indian during the campaign was on a night when he had to restrain his own men from butchering a more or less friendly Indian who was carrying a military pass. It could be said that Lincoln's personal contribution to the war against the Indians was that there was one more Indian alive at the end of it than there would have been if he hadn't taken up arms.

Some years later, while Lincoln was a representative in Congress (1847–1849), General Lewis Cass was a candidate for the Presidency, and his supporters were trying to endow him with a great military record. Mr. Lincoln spoke to the point as follows:

"By the way, Mr. Speaker, did you know I was a military hero? Yes, Sir, in the days of the Black Hawk war I fought, bled, and came away. General Cass's career in that war reminds me of my own.

13

NATIONAL REPUBLICAN CHART

A map, the party platform, pictures of former Presidents, and even Lincoln anecdotes appeared on 1860 campaign posters. In the center, framed by split rail fences, were the candidates: Abraham Lincoln and his running mate, Hannibal Hamlin.

"I was not at Stillman's defeat, but I was about as near it as Cass to Hull's surrender; and like him, I saw the place pretty soon afterwards.

"It is quite certain that I did not break my sword, for I had none to break, but I bent my musket pretty badly on one occasion. If General Cass went in advance of me picking whortleberries, I guess I surpassed him in charging upon the wild onion.

"If he saw any live, fighting Indians, it was more than I did, but I had a good many bloody struggles with the mosquitoes, and although I never fainted from lack of blood, I can truly say that I was often very hungry."

When Lincoln got back to New Salem after the war ended, only a few days were left before the 1832 election, but he did what campaigning he could. When the vote was counted it showed Lincoln getting 277 votes out of 300 in New Salem precinct, but it fell short of winning the election for him.

Writing about himself in the third person, he described his situation after the election in this way: "He was now without means and out of business, but anxious to remain with his friends who had treated him with so much generosity, especially as he had nothing elsewhere to go to. He studied what he should do; thought of learning the blacksmith trade, thought of trying to study law, rather thought he could not succeed at that without a better education."

Abe knew something about keeping a store and the Herndon Brothers' store was for sale. Using promissory notes, good will, and almost no cash, Abe and his friend William Berry bought it. They stocked up with merchandise from two other stores that had come on bad days—Reuben Bradford's and James Rutledge's.

Things might have worked out if one of Abe's first acts as a salesman had not been to buy a large barrel full of odds and ends that a westward-bound family didn't want to bother to lug any farther. In the bottom of the barrel the young storekeeper found a complete edition of Blackstone's *Commentaries,* the indispensable cornerstone of a lawyer's education.

"I began to read those famous works, and I had plenty of time; for during the long summer days when the farmers were busy with their crops, my customers were few and far between. The more I read, the more intensely interested I became. Never in my whole life was my mind so thoroughly absorbed. I read until I devoured them."

While the student was devouring his textbooks, his partners were drinking up the inventory and signing promissory notes. He added the job of postmaster to his chores and walked miles, delivering letters and newspapers which he carried in his hat. The best part of his job was that he got to read the papers before he delivered them.

One day he was stopped on his rounds by an elderly and unlettered Irishman, who asked Abe whether there was a letter for him.

"What's your name?" Abe asked.

The Irishman scratched his head. "Sure, it'll be on the letter," he said.

Blackstone taught Abe the rules of evidence quickly. One day a farmer came into the store and asked for a pair of buckskin gloves. Abe said he didn't have a pair of buckskin gloves but he had a good pair of dogskin gloves. The farmer had never heard of dogskin gloves, and asked Lincoln how he knew for sure that the gloves were made of dogskin. Abe's answer was judicial:

"I'll tell you how I know. Jack Clary's dog killed Tom Watkins' sheep, and Tom Watkins' boy killed the dog. Old John Mounts tanned the dog's skin and Sally Spears made the gloves. That's the way I know they're made of dogskin."

Finally the store failed and, after assuming debts that took him many years to pay, Abe walked the twenty miles to Springfield to see John Calhoun, a surveyor who had said he needed deputies. Abe located copies of Flint's and Gibson's treatises on surveying and walked home. After six weeks of study that left him haggard and exhausted, he went back to Springfield and announced himself ready for service.

He was a good surveyor, painstakingly accurate. The only mistakes he made were ones he made on purpose. Thirty years or so after he made a survey for the town of Petersburg, Illinois, some of the property owners were having trouble proving their boundaries. Finally an elderly man, hearing the argument, claimed he knew how it happened.

"I can tell you all about it. I helped carry the chain when Abe Lincoln laid out this town. Over there where they are quarrelling about the lines, when he was locating the street, he straightened up and said, 'If I run that street right through, it will cut three or four feet off the end of ——'s house. It's all he's got in the world and he never could get another. I reckon it won't hurt anything out here if I skew the line a little and miss him.' "

His career as a surveyor served his political interests well, and in 1834 he ran for the legislature again.

Jack and Hannah Armstrong had opened their home to him. According to Hannah, "Abe would come out to our house, drink milk, eat mush, corn-bread and butter, bring the children candy, and rock the cradle while I got something to eat . . . He would tell stories, joke people, boys and girls at parties. He would nurse babies—do anything to accommodate anybody."

Whenever the people of Lincoln's neighborhood engaged in a dispute; whenever a bet was to be decided, when they differed on points of religion or politics, when they wanted to get out of trouble or wanted advice on almost anything, they went to Abe.

After arguing for hours over the problem of how long a man's legs should be in proportion to the size of his body, two men came to Lincoln one day and asked for a judgment. Lincoln listened carefully to the contestants, pondered the matter, and handed down the following opinion:

"This question has been a source of controversy for untold

A Republican placard, 1860. Campaigners concentrated on such themes as their candidate's honesty, his pioneer background, and his rise from obscurity.

ages, and it is about time it should be definitely decided. It has led to bloodshed in the past, and there is no reason to suppose it will not lead to the same in the future.

"After much thought and consideration, not to mention mental worry and anxiety, it is my opinion, all side issues being swept aside, that a man's lower limbs, in order to preserve harmony of proportion, should be at least long enough to reach from his body to the ground."

During the political campaign of 1834, Lincoln and his friend Robert L. Wilson were two members of the Whig group of candidates known as the "Long Nine," each of them being over six feet tall. Rival candidates customarily traveled the district together in a series of joint debates. Sometimes Lincoln, who had no carriage of his own, would ride with his opponent. At one debate he closed by saying: "I am too poor to own a carriage, but my friend has generously invited me to ride with him. I want you to vote for me if you will; but if not then vote for my opponent, for he is a fine man." This time he was elected, for the first of four consecutive terms.

[4]

Although James Rutledge had given up his grocery store, he and his family ran a tavern that was the center of much of the social life of New Salem. James was president of a debating society where Lincoln talked well and frequently. Rutledge's daughter Ann, slender and fair-haired, was deeply aware of Lincoln's feeling for her and they saw a great deal of each other. She was engaged to be married to a man who called himself James McNeil and who had gone back east on a mysterious errand. His letters became more and more infrequent and finally stopped coming completely. What the understanding was between Lincoln and Ann Rutledge is not truly known, but in August of 1835, after days of raging fever, she died and Lincoln was inconsolable.

Weeks passed before those who loved him could touch him with a hand or word of comfort. He spent hours at her grave, returning to say, "I can't stand to think of her out there alone. The rain and storm shan't beat on her grave."

But he was a legislator now, and he had made commitments, so he went back to work. His friend Wilson made a note about his frame of mind:

"Lincoln told me that although he appeared to enjoy life rapturously, still he was the victim of a terrible melancholy. He sought company and indulged in fun and hilarity without restraint or stint as to time; but, when by himself, he told me that he was so overcome by mental depression that he never dared carry a knife with him."

Abe couldn't keep his humor out of his political life. During one session of the legislature a new surveyor for Schuyler County was nominated. The nomination was immediately followed by an opposing resolution to the effect that the nomination be voided because the office was not vacant at the time the nomination was made.

Abe commented: "That if, as appeared to be the opinion of legal gentlemen, there was no danger of the new surveyor's ousting the old one so long as he persisted not to die—he would suggest the propriety of letting matters remain as they were, so that if the old surveyor should hereafter conclude to die, there would be a new one ready made without troubling the legislature."

In 1836 he wrote a letter to the *Sangamo Journal:* "In your paper of last Saturday, I see a communication over the signature of 'Many Voters,' in which the candidates who are announced in the Journal are called upon to 'show their hands.' Agreed. Here's mine!

"I go for all sharing the privileges of the government, who assist in bearing its burthens. Consequently I go for admitting all whites to the right of suffrage, who pay taxes or bear arms, (by no means excluding females).

"If elected, I shall consider the whole people of Sangamon my constituents, as well those that oppose, as those that support me.

"While acting as their representative, I shall be governed by their will, on all subjects upon which I have the means of knowing what their will is; and upon all others, I shall do what my own judgment teaches me will best advance their interests. Whether elected or not, I go for distributing the proceeds of the sales of the public lands to the several states, to enable our state, in common with others, to dig canals and construct rail roads, without borrowing money and paying interest on it.

"If alive on the first Monday in November, I shall vote for Hugh L. White for President."

At the end of the 1837 session of the legislature, Lincoln decided to move to Springfield and practice law. He was offered a partnership by his old friend John T. Stuart, who had soldiered with him against Black Hawk, and immediately plunged into a succession of cases, small and large, complex and simple, comic and tragic.

His office in Springfield was directly over the courtroom, and Lincoln could keep close track of what was going on down below by simply opening a trapdoor in the floor. On one occasion he heard abusive and offensive comments from a political meeting which was in progress. When the spectators threatened to attack the speaker, Lincoln dropped down through the trapdoor and rebuked the audience.

"Gentlemen," he said, "let us not disgrace the age and the

At home in Springfield. Unlike the candidates of today, Lincoln did comparatively little traveling during his campaigns for office. Except for a few public appearances, he spent most of the time in the two-story house on Eighth Street. Here, neighbors greet him after the debates with Senator Douglas.

country in which we live. This is a land where freedom of speech is guaranteed. Mr. Baker has a right to speak, and ought to be permitted to do so. I am here to protect him, and no man shall take him from this stand if I can prevent it."

In a case against a young officer who had been indicted for an assault upon an aged gentleman, Lincoln opened the case by saying: "This is an indictment against a soldier for assaulting an old man."

"Sir," the defendant interrupted, "I am no soldier. I am an officer."

"I beg your pardon," Abe said. "Gentlemen of the jury, this is an indictment against an officer, who is no soldier, for assaulting an old man."

On another occasion, when it turned out that his client had indulged in fraudulent practices, Lincoln walked out of the courtroom and refused to continue with the case. The judge sent a messenger directing him to return, but he refused.

"Tell the judge," he said to the messenger, "that my hands are dirty and I've gone to wash them."

In spite of behavior like this, he got along well with the circuit judges. With one of them he got into a discussion about horse-trading, and the discussion ended with an agreement that Lincoln and the judge would trade horses at nine o'clock the following morning. Both horses were to be unseen until the moment of the trade. Promptly at nine the judge appeared, leading the sorriest specimen of a horse ever seen in those parts. In a few moments Lincoln appeared, carrying a wooden sawhorse over his shoulder. He set down the sawhorse and inspected the judge's animal.

"Well, Judge," he said, "that's the first time I ever got the worst of it in a horse trade."

He told stories in court as illustrations for the benefit of the jury. While defending a man against an assault charge, Lincoln claimed it was more like self-defense, as in the case of a man he once knew who was walking down the road with a pitchfork and was attacked by a very fierce dog. In trying to ward off the dog's attacks he stuck the prongs of the pitchfork into the animal and killed him. According to Lincoln, the dialogue that followed went like this:

"What made you kill my dog?" said the farmer.

"What made your dog try to bite me?" the man answered.

"But why didn't you go after him with the other end of your pitchfork?"

"Why didn't he come after me with his other end?"

Many times during this period, however, he spoke most directly about his convictions: "I hope I am over-wary; but if I am not, there is even now something of ill omen among us. I mean the increasing disregard for law which pervades the country—the growing disposition to substitute the wild and furious passions in lieu of the sober judgment of courts, and the worse than savage mobs for the executive ministers of justice. Here then, is one point at which danger may be expected.

"The question recurs, 'How shall we fortify against it?' The answer is simple. Let every American, every lover of liberty, every well-wisher to his posterity, swear by the blood of the Revolution never to violate in the least particular the laws of the country, and never to tolerate their violation by others.

"When I so pressingly urge a strict observance of all the laws, let me not be understood as saying there are no bad laws, or that grievances may not arise for the redress of which no legal provisions have been made. I mean to say no such thing. But I do mean to say that although bad laws, if they exist, should be repealed as soon as possible, still, while they continue in force, for the sake of example, they should be religiously observed. So also in unprovided cases. If such arise, let proper legal provisions be made for them with the least possible delay, but till then let them, if not intolerable, be

24

The Republican party conducted a unified and organized campaign. In the north, Wide Awake Clubs carried torches and marched in zig-zag formation. Above, a torchlight parade through City Hall Square, New York City.

borne with. There is no grievance that is a fit object for redress by mob law."

Mr. Lincoln had interesting characteristics as a lawyer. He was against litigation as a matter of principle, and he charged the lowest fees he decently could. "Discourage litigation," he urged. "Persuade your neighbors to compromise whenever you can. Point out to them that the nominal winner is often a real loser—in fees, expenses, and waste of time."

He maintained this attitude to the degree that, when one well-to-do Springfield man threatened to get another lawyer if Lincoln would not press his suit in the amount of $2.50 against an impoverished young attorney, Lincoln agreed to prosecute the case for a fee of ten dollars, payable in advance. He sought out the victim, gave him half the fee, and escorted him to court where the man accepted judgment and paid the $2.50.

In response to a request from a New York firm for information as to the financial rating of one of his Springfield neighbors, Lincoln wrote the following:

"I am well acquainted with Mr. ——, and know his circumstances. First of all, he has a wife and baby; together they ought to be worth $50,000 to any man. Secondly, he has an office in which there is a table worth $1.50 and three chairs worth, say, $1.00. Last of all there is in one corner a large rat hole, which will bear looking into. Respectfully, A. Lincoln."

Another letter ran as follows: "As to real estate, we cannot attend to it. We are not real estate agents, we are lawyers. We recommend that you give the charge of it to Mr. Isaac S. Britton, a trustworthy man and one whom the Lord made on purpose for such business."

He wasn't always so generous with his recommendations, however; he was asked by one client whether a certain neighbor was a man of means.

"Well, I reckon he ought to be," Abe said; "he's about the meanest man in town."

26

Such examples of a lighthearted approach to practice not-withstanding, Lincoln left no one in doubt as to his deadly seriousness about the law. On hearing the charge that the practice of law was not compatible with integrity, he said: "Let no young man choosing the law for a calling succumb to that popular belief. If in your judgment you cannot be an honest lawyer, resolve to be honest without being a lawyer. Choose some other occupation rather than one in the choosing of which you do, in advance, consent to be a knave."

A young lawyer who studied in Lincoln's office testified that Lincoln had said no more than he meant. One day after Lincoln had listened to a prospective client's statement of his case, he said: "Well, you have a pretty good case in technical law, but a pretty bad one in equity and justice. You'll have to get some other fellow to win this case for you. I couldn't do it. All the time, while talking to the jury, I'd be thinking, 'Lincoln, you're a liar,' and I believe I should forget myself and say it out loud."

Another youthful attorney asked him one day if the county seat of Logan County had been named for him. "Well, it was named *after* I was," Abe replied.

He never wearied of bearing humor as a gift to his friends. He would tell about a case in which a man was on trial for killing sheep. Every time the judge asked the man whether he pleaded guilty or not guilty the man answered, "I stands mute." Understandably enough, the verdict went against him, but he was duly informed that he could appeal the verdict to a higher court, the Court of Errors. The convicted man thought for a minute and then observed, "If this here ain't a court of errors I'd like to know where you can find one."

Again, in the case of a man who was charged with mistreating a livery horse, one witness, testifying for the defendant, said, "When his company rides fast, he rides fast; when his company rides slow, he rides slow." The prosecuting attorney then asked how the man rode when he was alone. "I don't know," the witness answered, "I never was with him when he was alone."

Sometimes the court itself came in for something less than reverential treatment. One man upon hearing his sentence accused the court of everything from stupidity to perfidy. He was fined ten dollars for contempt and paid his fine with a twenty-dollar bill. When he was told the court couldn't make change he said, "Never mind the other ten dollars, I'll take it out in contempt."

Whenever he wasn't pleading a case, keeping his political fences in order, or building new ones, Lincoln chopped wood.

[5]

By 1839 the rising young lawyer was a frequent guest in one of the largest and most attractive houses in Springfield, owned by his friend Ninian W. Edwards. One of the "Long Nine," Edwards was the son of a former governor of Illinois and was married to a charming Kentucky girl whose maiden name had been Elizabeth Todd. In 1840 Elizabeth invited her younger sister Mary to come and live with them.

Mary Todd was attractive, well-educated, could speak French, and knew more about clothes and cosmetics than any girl in Springfield. Furthermore, she knew exactly what she wanted. Her sister commented: "Mary was quick, gay and, in the social world, the more brilliant of the sisters. She loved show and power, and was one of the most ambitious women I ever knew. She used to contend, when a girl, to her friends in Kentucky, that she was destined to marry a President. I have

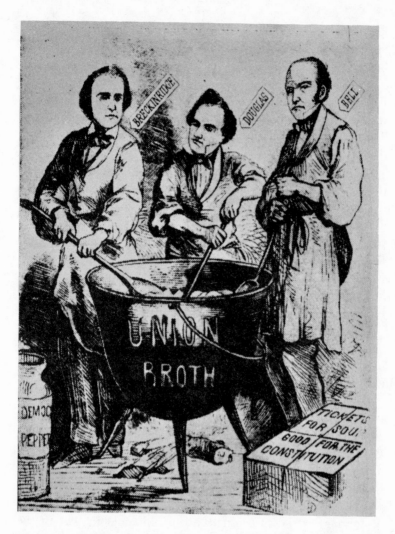

While Republicans had only one candidate to vote for, Democrats divided their loyalties among three—John C. Breckinridge of Kentucky, Stephen A. Douglas of Illinois, and John Bell of Tennessee.

heard her say that myself, and after mingling in society in Springfield, she repeated the seemingly absurd and idle boast."

At one of the parties she attended, she was introduced to Lincoln, who said he wanted to dance with her in the worst way. Miss Todd accepted, and after a few turns around the floor she sat down with one of her friends who had overheard the request.

"Well, Mary," the friend asked, "did he dance with you in the worst way?"

"Yes," Mary replied, "the very worst."

Another frequent guest at the Edwards' house was a stocky young lawyer formerly from Vermont, Stephen Arnold Douglas. Douglas had been state's attorney, member of the Illinois legislature, was register of the land office in Springfield, and was being spoken of more and more frequently as being a good man for the Democrats to send to Congress.

Lincoln knew Douglas well, had debated with him publicly on many issues, liked him, and didn't seem to be put out by the fact that Mary Todd seemed to be sizing them both up with more than a little interest.

One of Mary's friends once asked her jokingly which of the two she intended to marry. Without a moment's hesitation Mary replied, "The one who has the best chance of being President."

During the fall of 1840 it was accepted that Mary Todd was engaged to be married to Abraham Lincoln, and a story was circulated that the wedding would take place on the first of January, 1841. On that day Lincoln took his seat in the legislature and there was no wedding, even though, according to William H. Herndon, later Lincoln's law partner and one of his biographers, the guests had been invited and the wedding cake was in the oven. In reply to the question as to whether or not Mary had been left standing at the altar, her cousin wrote:

"There may have been a little shadow of foundation for Mr. Herndon's lively imagination to play upon, in that the year previous to their marriage and when Mr. Lincoln and my cousin Mary expected soon to be married, Mr. Lincoln was taken with one of those fearful, overwhelming periods of depression which induced his friends to persuade him to leave Springfield. This he did for a time; but I am satisfied that he was loyal and true to Mary, even though at times he may have doubted whether he was responding as fully as a manly, generous nature should to such affection as he knew my cousin was ready to bestow upon him. And this because it had not the overmastering depth of an early love."

One of Mary's sisters, Mrs. Wallace, when asked the same question said, "There is not a word of truth in it. I never was so amazed in my life as when I read that story. Mr. Lincoln never did such a thing."

Whatever the truth, Lincoln took the view that he had somehow treated Mary unforgivably, for in February he wrote his friend Joshua Speed, with whom he had shared a bed during the lean early days in Springfield: "Since then, it seems to me I should have been entirely happy, but for the never absent idea that there is one still unhappy whom I have contributed to make so. That still kills my soul. I cannot but reproach myself for even wishing to be happy while she is otherwise."

In spite of the doubts they apparently entertained about each other, they did not avoid each other's company. Mary had embraced Lincoln's political views and took up the Republicans' cause in the local newspaper.

The Auditor of the State of Illinois at that time was a fiery-tempered Democrat named James Shields. The finances of the state were in deplorable condition and Shields had refused to accept money issued by the State Bank in payment of taxes. The *Sangamo Journal* printed a letter of unknown authorship which, in a backwoods dialect, savagely ridiculed

Mr. Shields. This letter, signed "Rebecca," so delighted Mary Todd and her friend Julia Jayne that they wrote two more letters in a similar vein, also signed Rebecca. Lincoln knew about the two letters and saw no reason to try to hold them back.

When the State Auditor read the second composition of the two young ladies he reacted with an explosion heard all over the state. He called the editor of the paper and demanded to know who had written the letters. He was told that Mr. Lincoln assumed responsibility for the last two missives.

In due course a representative of Mr. Shields called upon Lincoln and in a somewhat pompous, though courtly, manner informed him that Mr. Shields had challenged Mr. Lincoln to a duel, and that, as the challenged party, it was Mr. Lincoln's right to choose the weapons. Refusing to believe that Mr. Shields' emissary was in earnest, Mr. Lincoln replied, "How about cow-dung at five paces?"

The response was hardly acceptable, and in the correspondence that followed Lincoln agreed, reluctantly, to meet his medium-sized opponent in a trial by combat. He chose cavalry sabers of the largest size. When the contestants and their retinues were assembled in the appointed place, Lincoln, having whooshed his sword around in the air, explained to Shields that the whole affair was political, and that he had not intended any personal affront or injury. Whether it was the sight of his huge, perfectly conditioned opponent carving the breeze with a saber, or whether it was the sincere and friendly wording of the explanation is uncertain; in any event Mr. Shields relaxed and departed the field of honor in peace, having lost neither face nor limb.

Lincoln's own code regarding matters like this was clearly stated to a young officer who had been court-martialed for having a quarrel with a brother officer.

"Quarrel not at all. No man resolved to make the most of

himself, can spare time for personal contention. Still less can he afford to take all the consequences, including the vitiating of his temper, and the loss of self-control. Yield larger things to which you can show no more than equal right; and yield lesser ones, though clearly your own. Better give your path to a dog, than be bitten by him in contesting the right. Even killing the dog would not cure the bite."

On the other hand, when he believed himself to be in the right, he fought, and fought hard. Upon winning a long and complicated two-year case for the Illinois Central, he submitted a bill for two thousand dollars. An official of the railroad looked at the bill and said, "We cannot allow such a claim; why, Sir, this is as much as Daniel Webster himself would have charged." Lincoln withdrew the bill and filed suit for a five-thousand-dollar fee. At the trial six lawyers testified that the fee was reasonable, and the charge was allowed.

Lincoln's reputation as an effective and popular, rough-and-tumble politician was growing, and in the presidential campaign of 1840 he worked tirelessly for the Whig candidate General William H. Harrison and rejoiced in the success of "Old Tippecanoe."

After almost two years of doubt and misunderstanding, Mary Todd and Abraham Lincoln were married suddenly on November 4, 1842. The marriage was one of the first in Springfield to be celebrated with all the ceremony of the Episcopal Church. One of Lincoln's friends, Justice Thomas C. Browne, grew fidgety during the formalities. When the bridegroom repeated the words: "With this ring I thee wed and with all my worldly goods I thee endow," the judge exclaimed, "Grace to Goshen, Lincoln, the statute fixes all that."

One witness reported that Lincoln, speaking out of the corner of his mouth to the judge, said, "I just thought I'd add a little dignity to the statute."

The newly married couple did not set up an elaborate household. They went to live at the Globe Tavern, where

Four candidates for President dance to music played by a Negro slave—Dred Scott. Although Scott had lost his fight for freedom three years earlier, his case provided explosive issues for the 1860 campaign.

they paid four dollars a week for room and board. He wrote Speed, "I most heartily wish you and your family will not fail to come. Just let us know the time, a week in advance, and we will have a room prepared for you, and will all be merry together for a while."

[6]

Lincoln had been a member of the General Assembly of Illinois since 1834. He felt now that he should seek a higher office, and so did many of his friends. In 1841 pressure had been put upon him to run for the governorship, but he declined. In 1843, soon after the birth of his first son, Robert, he announced himself to be a candidate for Congress, but his party had other plans. "It would astonish, if not amuse, the older citizens," he wrote, "to learn that I have been put down here as the candidate of pride, wealth and aristocratic family distinction."

The months passed swiftly. Lincoln's law partnership with Judge Stephen T. Logan made it possible for Mr. and Mrs. Lincoln and their son Robert to live in a one-story frame house of their own. Lincoln was away a great deal of time indefatigably practicing his two professions: law and politics.

Life in the circuit courts went on as usual. Judge Lawrence Weldon reported that one day a lawyer challenged a juror because of his personal acquaintance with Mr. Lincoln, who was appearing for the other side. Such an objection was somewhat a reflection on the honor of a lawyer, and Judge David Davis, who was presiding at the time, promptly overruled the challenge. When Lincoln followed his opponent's lead and began to ask the talesmen whether they were acquainted with his opponent, and two or three answered in the affirmative, Judge Davis observed:

"Now, Mr. Lincoln, you are wasting time. The mere fact that a juror knows your opponent does not disqualify him."

"No, your honor," Lincoln replied. "But I'm afraid some of the gentlemen *don't* know him, which would place me at a disadvantage."

In response to a glib but shallow summation of a case on the part of an opposing lawyer, Mr. Lincoln addressed the jury as follows:

"His habit—of which you have witnessed a very painful specimen in his argument to you in this case—of reckless assertion and statement without grounds, need not be imputed to him as a moral fault or blemish. He can't help it. For reasons which, gentlemen of the jury, you and I have not time to study here, as deplorable as they are surprising, the oratory of the gentleman completely suspends all action of his mind. The moment he begins to talk, his mental operations cease. I never knew of but one thing which compared to my friend in this particular. That was a steamboat. Back in the days when I performed my part as a keel-boatman, I made the acquaintance of a trifling little steamboat which used to bustle and puff and wheeze about the Sangamon River. It had a five-foot boiler and a seven-foot whistle, and every time it whistled, the boat stopped."

Lincoln and Judge Davis had many exchanges over the years. Jesse Weik, a close friend and associate of Lincoln and Herndon, wrote of a man who tracked Lincoln with a letter of recommendation to a tavern in the town of Danville and found him in an upstairs bedroom having a pillow fight with the 300-pound judge.

In one such tavern, on a bitter winter night, Lincoln joined a group of fellow lawyers in front of the fireplace.

"Pretty cold night," one man commented.

"Colder than hell," Lincoln replied.

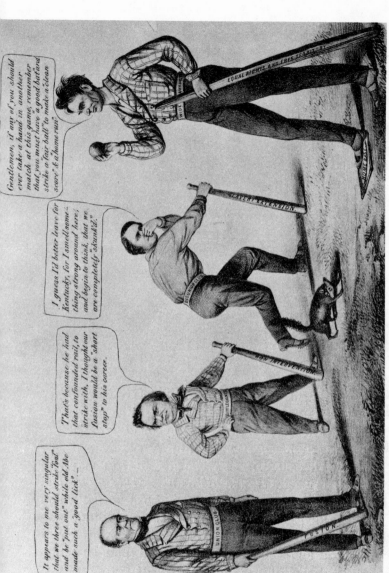

With four candidates, Lincoln emerged triumphant. This Currier and Ives cartoon shows him "skunking" Democrats Bell, Douglas, and Breckinridge in a political baseball game.

A colleague turned to him and said, "You've been there, Mr. Lincoln?"

"Oh, yes," Lincoln replied, "and the funny thing is that it's much like it is here—all the lawyers are nearest the fire."

The courts were not as formally run in those days, and Lincoln, when not busy, used to whisper stories to his friends to the intense annoyance of Judge Davis. When the monologues and smothered laughter had gone on too long, the judge would pound his gavel and say:

"Come, come, Mr. Lincoln, I can't stand this. There is no use trying to carry on two courts; I must adjourn mine or you yours, and I think you will have to be the one."

As soon as the court adjourned the judge would call one of the men and say, "What was that Lincoln was saying?"

"I was never fined but once for contempt of court," said one of the clerks of the Eighth Circuit. "Davis fined me five dollars. Mr. Lincoln had just come in, and, leaning over my desk, told me a story so irresistibly funny that I broke out in a loud laugh. The judge called me to order. 'This must be stopped. You and Mr. Lincoln are constantly disturbing the court with your stories.' Then he instructed me to fine myself five dollars. I apologized, but said the story was worth five dollars. After the session the judge asked me to tell him the story, and I did. 'Remit your fine,' he ordered."

In writing about Lincoln's way with humor, Herndon said, "In the role of a story-teller I regard Mr. Lincoln as without an equal. His power of mimicry and his manner of recital were unique. His countenance and all his features seemed to take part in the performance. As he neared the pith or point of the story every vestige of seriousness disappeared from his face. His gray eyes sparkled; a smile seemed to gather up, curtain-like, the corners of his mouth; his frame quivered with suppressed excitement; and when the nub of the story— as he called it—came, no one's laugh was heartier than his."

A lawyer opposed to Lincoln tried to convince a jury that precedent was superior to law, and that custom made things legal in all cases. When Lincoln rose to answer him, he told the jury he would argue his case in the same way:

"Old Squire Bagly, from Menard, came into my office and said, 'Lincoln, I want your advice as a lawyer. Has a man what's been elected Justice of the Peace a right to issue a marriage license?' I told him he had not; then the old squire threw himself back in his seat and said very indignantly, 'Lincoln, I thought you was a lawyer. Now Bob Thomas and I had a bet on this thing and we agreed to let you decide; but if this is your opinion I don't want it, for I know a thundering sight better. I been squire now eight years and have done it all the time.' "

Lincoln's story-telling began to be used against him by his political opponents, who tried to create the image of a jester who would go to any lengths to get a laugh. Frederick Trevor Hill, a lawyer who wrote in depth of Lincoln's career as a lawyer, commented:

"Nothing can be more absurd than to picture Lincoln as a combination of buffoon and drummer. He was frequently the life of our little company, keeping us good-natured, making us see the funny side of things and generally entertaining us; but to create the impression that the circuit was a circus of which Lincoln was the clown is ridiculous."

Mr. Hill wrote of another friend who was of the same mind.

"In all my experience I never heard Lincoln tell a story for its own sake or simply to raise a laugh. He used stories to illustrate a point, but the idea that he sat around and matched yarns like a commercial traveler is utterly false."

"Lincoln would soon have become a bore if he traded on his story-telling gifts," another friend said; "he traveled with the same men day after day and month after month. Even if his fund of anecdotes could have stood the strain, we should not have been able to endure it, for no man exhausts himself or others so quickly as the professional funny man."

One of Lincoln's favorite places of relaxation in Springfield was a general store, where he would sit by the hour passing the time with friends. The storekeeper, to whom Ida M. Tarbell, one of Lincoln's biographers, gave the name Billy Brown, said:

"Tell stories? Nobody ever could beat him at that, and how he'd enjoy them, just slap his hands on his knees and jump up and turn around and then set down, laughing to kill. Ever hear Judge Weldon tell that story about what Lincoln said one day up to Bloomington when they was takin' up a subscription to buy Ward Lamon a new pair of pants? No? Well, perhaps I oughten to tell it to you, Ma says it ain't nice."

According to witnesses, what Lincoln said with considerable gravity was: "I cannot contribute to the end in view."

"It makes me mad to hear people objectin' to Mr. Lincoln's stories," Billy Brown continued; "mebbe he did say words you wouldn't expect to hear at a church supper, but he never put no meaning into them that wouldn't a been fit for the minister to put into a sermon, and that's a blamed sight more'n you can say of a lot of stories I've heard some of the people tell who stick up their noses at Mr. Lincoln's yarns."

[7]

In 1846, Lincoln ran for Congress. His opponent was Peter Cartwright, a circuit-riding evangelist with a large following. Lincoln campaigned hard, and the current seemed to be with him. The Democrats brought up everything they could think of against him, including many references to his being married to a "high-toned Episcopalian." He was accused of being a deist, who believed in God, perhaps, but did not accept Christ and doctrines of atonement and punishment.

Lincoln, who once said, "When I do good I feel good, and when I do bad I feel bad, that's my religion," attended a religious meeting at which Cartwright was to speak. And speak he did, exhorting, waving his arms, and shouting prayers. Finally, he quieted down and said, "All who desire to lead a new life, to give their hearts to God and go to Heaven, will stand." A few men and women and children rose to their feet. Then Cartwright went on, "All who do not wish to go to hell will stand." At this point everybody in the meeting hall stood up except Lincoln. Transfixing Lincoln with his burning eyes, Cartwright said, "I observe that many responded to the first invitation to give their hearts to God and go to Heaven. And I further observe that all of you save one indicated that you do not desire to go to hell. The sole exception is Mr. Lincoln, who did not respond to either invitation. May I inquire of you, Mr. Lincoln, where are you going?"

Lincoln rose and spoke quietly: "I came here as a respectful listener. I did not know I was going to be singled out by Brother Cartwright. I believe in treating religious matters with due solemnity. I admit that the questions propounded by Brother Cartwright are of great importance. I did not feel called upon to answer as the rest did. Brother Cartwright asks me directly where I am going. I desire to reply with equal directness. I am going to Congress."

Lincoln won the election with a fifteen-hundred-vote plurality, and one of his first acts after the ballots had been counted was to account for his campaign funds. A group of friends had raised $200 for his expenses, of which he returned $199.25, with the following message: "I did not need the money. I made the canvass on my own horse; my entertain-

UNCLE SAM" MAKING NEW ARRANGEMENTS.

According to one cartoonist, Uncle Sam was looking for an "honest, upright, capa-

ment, being at the houses of my friends, cost me nothing. My only outlay was 75 cents for a barrel of cider which some farmhands insisted I should treat to."

When he left for Washington in 1847 to take up his duties as a freshman Congressman he said goodbye to Mary, Robert, and a new son, Edward.

The whole country was excited over the Mexican War. As Lincoln and the Whigs saw it, President Polk had acted as Frederick the Great had in Silesia: "Take possession first and negotiate afterwards." The Whigs voted again and again that the war was "unnecessarily and unconstitutionally commenced by the president." But Whigs joined Democrats in voting supplies needed to win the war. Lincoln's opposition to the war was well known, and his attitude was not welcomed by many of the voters who had elected him. There was a new brand of military hero in the country, and the country wanted him. Lincoln listened to congressional utterances on the subject until he was weary.

He commented once after listening to a lengthy speech on the subject, "I never saw so many words compressed into so small an idea."

The whole affair reminded him of the farmer who said, "I ain't greedy for land, all I want is what joins mine."

He had great respect for words and took care in using them. "I shall never be old enough," Lincoln said, "to speak without embarrassment when I have nothing to talk about."

In the fall of 1848 he toured New England, where he made a notable and lasting impression. On the way home he took the Erie Canal route to Buffalo and visited Niagara Falls. When Herndon asked what impressed him most about the Falls Lincoln answered. "The thing that struck me most forcibly was, where in the world did all that water come from?"

At the end of one term as a congressman his party decided not to put Lincoln up for a second. He returned to Springfield pondering a political career that, contrary to natural law, had more downs than ups.

He became a familiar figure on the streets of his home town again. When he took his boys for walks, it was customary for one of them to be mounted on his shoulder while the other clung to the tails of his long coat. One day they were making their way home in this manner with both boys screaming at the top of their lungs. A passer-by asked Lincoln what was wrong with them.

Lincoln smiled and answered, "Just what's the matter with the whole world. I've got three walnuts and each wants two."

"From 1849 to 1854, both inclusive," Lincoln wrote, "practiced law more assiduously than ever before. . . . I was losing interest in politics, when the repeal of the Missouri Compromise aroused me again."

The Kansas-Nebraska Act left the matter of slavery up to local or "squatter" sovereignty, and the issue became a barrier across the course of the developing nation.

Lincoln had many arguments about the matter with his colleagues, taking the position that one day slavery must become extinct. After one such discussion Judge T. Lyle Dickey wrote:

"After a while we went upstairs to bed. There were two beds in our room, and I remember that Lincoln sat up in his nightshirt on the edge of the bed arguing the point with me. At last we went to sleep. Early in the morning I woke up and there was Lincoln half sitting up in bed.

" 'Dickey,' he said, 'I tell you this nation cannot exist half slave and half free.'

" 'Oh, Lincoln,' said I, 'go to sleep.' "

On one occasion Lincoln spoke directly to the point:

"*Most governments* have been based, practically, on the denial of equal rights of men, as I have, in part, stated them; *ours* began by *affirming* these rights. *They* said, some men are too *ignorant*, and *vicious*, to share in government. Possi-

44

bly so, said we; and, by your system, you would always keep them ignorant, and vicious.

"If A. can prove, however conclusively, that he may, of right, enslave B.—why may not B. snatch the same argument, and prove equally, that he may enslave A.?—

"You say A. is white, and B. is black. It is *color*, then; the lighter, having the right to enslave the darker? Take care. By this rule, you are to be slave to the first man you meet, with a fairer skin than your own.

"You do not mean *color* exactly?—You mean the whites are *intellectually* the superiors of the blacks, and, therefore, have a right to enslave them? Take care again. By this rule, you are to be slave to the first man you meet, with an intellect superior to your own.

"But, you say, it is a question of *interest*; and, if you can make it your *interest,* you have the right to enslave another. Very well. And if he can make it his interest, he has the right to enslave you."

As far as the slaveholder's attitude toward slavery went, Mr. Lincoln said he understood it perfectly. It reminded him of something a boyhood friend of his said about skinning eels. "It doesn't hurt them so very much. It's been going on for a long time, they're used to it."

[8]

Lincoln was very conscious of his personal appearance and frequently made jokes about it. Many times he appropriated the story about a stranger approaching an ugly man and offering him a gift, saying that he had made a promise that if he ever met a man uglier than himself he would give him the gift. Another version ran as follows:

"One day when I first came here (Springfield) I got into a fit of musing in my room and stood resting my elbows on the bureau. Looking into the glass, it struck me what an ugly man I was. The fact grew on me and I made up my mind that I must be the ugliest man in the world. It so maddened me that I resolved, should I ever see an uglier, I would shoot him on sight. Not long after this Archie"—naming a lawyer present—"came to town and the first time I saw him I said to myself, 'There's the man.' I went home, took down my gun, and prowled the streets waiting for him. He soon came along. 'Halt, Archie,' said I, pointing the gun at him, 'say your prayers, for I am going to shoot you.' 'Why, Mr. Lincoln, what's the matter, what have I done?' 'Well, I made an oath that if I ever saw an uglier man than I am, I'd shoot him on the spot. You are uglier, so make ready to die.' 'Mr. Lincoln, do you really think I am uglier than you?' 'Yes.' 'Well, Mr. Lincoln,' said Archie deliberately, and looking me squarely in the face, 'if I am any uglier, fire away.' "

One variant of this story he used in a meeting of newspaper editors, where he felt out of place. "I feel like I did once when I met a woman riding horseback in the woods. As I stopped to let her pass, she also stopped and looking at me intently, said, 'I do believe you are the ugliest man I ever saw.' Said I: 'Madam, you are probably right, but I can't help it.'

" 'No,' she said, 'you can't help it, but you might stay at home.' "

He was careless in his dress, and the same thing might have been said about his office paperwork. He owned a large desk-bookcase, but his real working file was his tall silk hat, where he kept most of his important business papers and memoranda. In writing to a fellow lawyer whose correspondence he had neglected, Lincoln said,

"When I received the letter, I put it in my hat, and, buying a new one the next day, the old one was set aside, and so the letter was lost sight of for a time."

He once left his hat on a chair, and a lady of considerable proportions sat on it. When she arose, Lincoln said: "Madam, I could have told you it wouldn't have fitted."

On top of his desk there was usually a bundle of miscellaneous papers with a note on it saying, "When you cannot find *it* anywhere else, look into this."

If things were sometimes difficult to find in the Lincoln house it was, perhaps, understandable, for Robert and Edward Lincoln now had two little brothers—William Wallace, born in 1850 and Tad in 1853.

In 1855 Lincoln for the first time met a man who was to be profoundly identified with him in later years. The man was a brilliant Ohio lawyer, Edwin M. Stanton. At a trial in Cincinnati, the attorney for the defense chose Stanton instead of Lincoln to make the forensic address to the jury. Lincoln was disappointed at the choice, and his bitterness was intensified by Stanton's references to him as "a long, lank creature from Illinois, wearing a dirty linen duster for a coat, on the back of which the perspiration had splotched wide stains that resembled the map of the continent." Lincoln himself overheard Stanton saying, "Where did that long-armed creature come from, and what can he expect to do in this case?"

Lincoln observed, "I have never been so brutally treated as by that man Stanton."

In May, 1856, Lincoln delivered one of his most impressive speeches at the first Republican state convention in Bloomington, Illinois. This famous "lost" speech, of which there appears to be no accurate transcript, so moved John L. Scripps that he wrote to the *Chicago Tribune*: "Again and again during its delivery they sprang to their feet and upon the benches and testified, by long continued shouts and waving of hats, how deeply the speaker had wrought upon their minds and hearts."

On the advice of eleven-year-old Grace Bedell, who felt that "all the ladies like whiskers," the candidate allowed his to grow. The beard may or may not have won votes, but it did start a new fashion.

As Lincoln left the platform after his extraordinary and moving performance, Jesse K. Dubois, who had been nominated State Auditor, turned to Henry Whitney, a lawyer and a friend of Lincoln's from the Eighth Circuit days, saying, "That is the greatest speech ever made in Illinois and puts Lincoln on the track for the Presidency."

Twenty days later the delegates to the first national Republican convention met in Philadelphia to nominate candidates for President and Vice-President.

At the time of the convention Lincoln was in Urbana at a special term of court conducted by his old friend Judge Davis. The judge and the nonresident lawyers were all staying at a local hotel where their sleep was shattered early every morning by the sound of a loud gong. The visiting members of the legal fraternity decided that the gong must be removed, and Lincoln was unanimously elected to perform the operation. The following morning he left the courtroom early, slipped into the dining room, picked up the gong, hid it under his coat, and started to leave. On the way out the door he was met by Judge Davis and Henry Whitney. Whitney had a copy of the *Chicago Tribune* which had just reached town, and announced the surprising news that the Philadelphia convention had given Lincoln 110 votes for the Vice-Presidency.

Davis looked at the bulge under Lincoln's coat. "Great business this," he said, "for a man who aspires to be Vice-President of the United States."

Lincoln smiled. "Surely it ain't me," he said; "there's another man named Lincoln down in Massachusetts. I reckon it's him."

On the sixteenth of June, 1858, the Republican state convention passed a unanimous resolution declaring Abraham Lincoln to be "the first and only choice of the Republicans of Illinois for the United States Senate as the successor of Stephen A. Douglas."

Stephen Douglas had been elected to the United States Senate in 1847 and was becoming the celebrated leader of the movement to leave all questions regarding slavery up to local authority.

The night of his nomination Lincoln delivered his famous "house divided" speech. In more ways than one the speech was a direct challenge to his familiar and respected adversary.

Soon afterward Lincoln forced Douglas into agreeing to a series of debates. Douglas knew what he was letting himself in for.

"I do not feel," he told his friends, "that I want to go into this debate. The whole country knows me and has me measured. Lincoln, as regards myself, is comparatively unknown, and if he gets the best of this debate—and I want to say that he is the ablest man the Republicans have got—I shall lose everything and Lincoln will gain everything. Should I win, I shall gain but little. I do not want to go into debate with Abe."

No one recognized more clearly than Lincoln the difference between himself and his opponent. "With me," he said sadly, "the race of ambition has been a failure, a flat failure. With him it has been one of splendid success."

At Springfield in July he elaborated on the career of his opponent. "Senator Douglas is of world-wide renown. All the anxious politicians of the party, or who have been of his party for years past, have been looking upon him as certainly, at no distant day, to be the President of the United States. They have seen in his round, jolly, fruitful face, postoffices, landoffices, marshalships, and cabinet appointments, charge-ships and foreign missions, bursting and sprouting out in wonderful exuberance. . . . *We* have to fight this battle upon principle, and upon principle alone."

From the beginning it was evident that the central issue of the debates was to be the implications of the Dred Scott decision. Scott was a Negro, whose Missouri master had moved to

"I see a storm coming," the candidate had said during the campaign. Soon after his election the Southern states seceded from the Union and took over arsenals in their territory. In this cartoon the President-elect perches uncomfortably on a seat of bayonets.

the free state of Illinois, then to the free territory of Wisconsin, and then back to Missouri, where Scott was sold. Scott filed suit in a Missouri court to establish his freedom, claiming that his residence in free territories had emancipated him. The local court found in his favor, but the court of appeals reversed the decision. Scott was then sold again and filed suit in the federal court of St. Louis, which ruled against him. The case was then appealed to the United States Supreme Court, which handed down a verdict to the effect that slave-owners could enjoy their property *wherever situated* as a constitutional right. In effect, as Lincoln put it, "If any man chose to enslave another, no third man shall be allowed to object."

Lincoln was dead-set against any extension of slavery, and he was dead-set against the Supreme Court ruling that permitted such extension. He fought hard.

In a series of debates still unrivaled in American politics, the "long and the short of it" battled each other head to head across Illinois. About the debates David R. Locke, an Ohio newspaperman, reported: "Douglas was the demagogue all the way through. There was no trick of presentation he did not use. He suppressed facts, twisted conclusion, and perverted history. He wriggled and turned, and dodged; he appealed to prejudices; in short, it was evident that what he was laboring for was Douglas and nothing else. . . . Lincoln on the other hand, kept strictly to the questions at issue, and no one could doubt but that the cause for which he was speaking was the only thing he had at heart; that his personal interests did not weigh a particle. . . . He knew that the people had the intelligence to strike the average correctly. His great strength was in trusting the people instead of considering them as babes in arms."

Lincoln and Locke met in Quincy, and Lincoln was attracted to the young reporter who was destined, under the name of Petroleum V. Nasby, to become one of Lincoln's, and the nation's, favorite humorists. The two men talked of a number of things in that first meeting, including the recent death of a military figure who was held in high esteem by his countrymen and by himself.

"If the General had known how big a funeral he was going to have," Lincoln said, "he would have died years ago."

At the time the boundlessly ambitious George B. McClellan, who was later to oppose Lincoln so fiercely, was vice-president of the Illinois Central Railroad, and out of his political persuasion provided a special train with a private car for the campaigning Douglas.

As the candidates hurried to the southern part of the state for one of their debates, Lincoln was traveling in the caboose of a freight train which was sidetracked to allow the Douglas special to go through. The Douglas train, decorated with banners and flags, carried a brass band which was playing "Hail to the Chief." As the train whistled past, Lincoln laughed and said, "Boys, the gentleman in that car evidently smelt no royalty in our carriage."

One lady who followed the debates commented that after Douglas spoke she was sorry for Lincoln, and after Lincoln spoke she was sorry for Douglas.

She needn't have felt sorry for Mr. Lincoln, for he was no newcomer to trial by combat in the political arena. In the second debate, he forced Douglas into answering the one question that Douglas didn't want to answer. This was the question: "Can the people of a United States Territory, in any lawful way, against the wish of any citizen of the United States, exclude slavery from its limits?"

Lincoln's friends had advised him not to ask the question because they felt it would assure Douglas's election to the Senate, if he answered in the affirmative.

"If he does that," said Mr. Lincoln, "he can never be President. I am after larger game; the battle of 1860 is worth a hundred of this."

Douglas's dilemma, as explained by Frederick Trevor Hill, was as follows: If he replied in the negative, reassuring the slave-owners, the people of free Illinois would reject him, on the grounds that slavery by the Dred Scott decision had already been forced upon the territories. If Douglas answered in the affirmative, he would forever alienate the Southern Democrats.

Douglas answered the question in the affirmative: ". . . the people have the lawful means to introduce it (slavery) or exclude it as they please, for the reason that slavery cannot exist a day or an hour anywhere, unless it is supported by local police regulations."

The wedge had been driven, and the Democratic Party in the United States fatally split.

In one debate Douglas hammered away at certain statements of Senator Lyman Trumbull to which Lincoln had subscribed. Senator Trumbull was a favorite target for the Democrats. He had been elected to the House of Representatives on the Democratic ticket in 1854. He was advanced to the Senate before Congress convened, and then turned Republican and became a dedicated supporter of Lincoln. The Trumbull statements were lies, Douglas declaimed. In answer, Lincoln said:

"Why, sir, there is not one single statement in Trumbull's speech that depends on Trumbull's veracity. Why does not Judge Douglas answer the facts? If you have studied geometry, you remember that by a course of reasoning Euclid proves that all the angles in a triangle are equal to two right angles. Euclid has shown how to work it out. Now if you undertook to disprove that proposition, to prove that it was erroneous, could you do that by calling Euclid a liar?"

Lincoln commented that Douglas's reasoning was "as thin as the homoeopathic soup that was made by boiling the shadow of a pigeon that had been starved to death."

"Judge Douglas," Lincoln said, "is playing cuttlefish—a

After the election, South Carolina was the first state to leave the Union. Louisiana, Mississippi, Alabama, Florida, and Georgia followed close behind.

small species of fish that has no mode of defending itself when pursued except by throwing out a black fluid which makes the water so dark the enemy cannot see it; and thus escapes."

During the Charleston debate Douglas accused Lincoln of having, while in Congress, voted against the appropriation for supplies to be sent the United States soldiers in Mexico.

This was a perversion of the facts, Lincoln claimed. He was opposed to the policy of the administration in declaring war against Mexico; but when war was declared he never failed to vote for the support of any proposition looking to the comfort of the men who were maintaining the dignity of our flag in a war Lincoln thought unnecessary and unjust.

He gradually became more excited, and looking around as if for corroboration, saw that O. B. Ficklin, a Douglas man, was seated on the stand. Lincoln reached back, grabbed Ficklin by the collar of his coat, lifted him from his seat, and roared, "Fellow citizens, here is Ficklin, who was at the time in Congress with me, and he knows it's a lie."

After the meeting was over, Ficklin, who, in spite of being a Democrat, was a warm friend of Lincoln's, said: "Lincoln, you damn near shook all the Democracy out of me today."

Thomas H. Tibbles wrote of one debate, "Judge Douglas closed his speech with a very bitter attack upon Lincoln's career. He said Lincoln had tried everything and had always been a failure. He had tried farming and failed at that, had tried flatboating and failed at that, had tried school-teaching and failed at that, had sold liquor in a saloon and failed at that, had tried law and failed at that, and now he had gone into politics and was doomed to make the worst failure of all.

"That part of Judge Douglas's speech," Tibbles continued, "aroused my anger to white heat, and I was provoked at Lincoln as he sat there, and laughed during its delivery. He seemed greatly amused by it. At length he rose to reply. He came forward and said that he was very much obliged to

Judge Douglas for the very accurate history that he had taken the trouble to compile. It was all true, every word of it. 'I have,' said Lincoln, 'worked on a farm; I have split rails; I have worked on a flatboat; I have tried to practice law. There is just one thing that Judge Douglas forgot to relate. He says that I sold liquor over a counter. He forgot to tell you that, while I was on one side of the counter, the Judge was always on the other.' "

Other people who were there said that when the roar of laughter had subsided, Lincoln added, "But since then I have quit the business."

Technically, the issue of the debates was the *extension* of slavery into the territories; but Lincoln, whenever he could, brought out the fact that he was concerned with the right or wrong of slavery.

"That," he said in the last debate, "is the real issue. That is the issue that will continue in this country when these poor tongues of Judge Douglas and myself shall be silent. It is the eternal struggle between these two principles—right and wrong—throughout the world. They are the two principles that have stood face to face from the beginning of time; and will ever continue to struggle. The one is the common right of humanity and the other the divine right of kings. It is the same principle in whatever shape it develops itself. It is the same spirit that says, 'You work and toil and earn bread, and I'll eat it.' No matter in what shape it comes, whether from the mouth of a king who seeks to bestride the people of his own nation and live by the fruit of their labor, or from one race of men as an apology for enslaving another race, it is the same tyrannical principle."

When the votes were counted in November, 1858, the Republicans received 125,430, Douglas Democrats, 121,607, and Lecompton Democrats, a splinter group so committed to slavery that they didn't think it was arguable, 5,071. However, it was the state legislature that cast the final vote, and the apportionment of districts was such that there was a majority for Douglas.

Lincoln took his defeat calmly. "I felt," he said, "like the boy that stumped his toe,—'it hurt too bad to laugh, and he was too big to cry.' " In a letter to Dr. A. G. Henry he wrote: "I am glad I made the late race. It gave me a hearing on the great and durable question of the age, which I would have had in no other way; and though I now sink out of view, and shall be forgotten, I believe I have made some marks which will tell for the cause of civil liberty long after I am gone."

The debates with Douglas had made Lincoln a national figure, and he was greatly in demand as a speaker. It is obvious that he was concerned that the cause of principle had been obscured by the rhetoric of the recent campaign, for in answer to an invitation to speak in Boston in honor of the birthday of Thomas Jefferson, he communicated his regret at not being able to make the address and added:

"I remember being once much amused at seeing two partially intoxicated men engaged in a fight with their great overcoats on, which fight, after a long and rather harmless contest, ended in each having fought himself out of his own coat and into that of the other. If the two leading parties of today are really identical with the two in the days of Jefferson and Adams, they have performed the feat of the two drunken men."

[9]

On Sunday, October 16, 1859, John Brown invaded Harpers Ferry and seized the United States Armory and Arsenal in the hope of sparking a slave insurrection. After thirty-six

Lincoln tried to prod his top general, George McClellan, to action and victory, but with little success. Here the General, as pictured by a cartoonist, sits in his headquarters at Harrison's Landing.

hours of confused and random fighting, ten of Brown's twenty-two men were dead; five had escaped; and Brown and the remaining seven had been subdued by a detachment of eighty Marines under the command of Brevet Colonel Robert E. Lee of the United States Army.

Lincoln felt that the raid was wrong for two reasons. It was a violation of the law, and it was, as all such attacks must be, futile as far as any effect it might have on the extinction of a great evil.

Brown was hanged on the second of December, and when Congress met, a few days later, the Senate appointed an investigating committee to inquire into the matter. Democratic Senators Jefferson Davis of Mississippi, James M. Mason of Virginia, and Graham N. Fitch of Indiana tried hard to find grounds for blaming the whole thing on the Republican party.

Soon after Brown was hanged, Lincoln accepted a paid invitation to speak at the famous Cooper Institute in New York. His audience was a distinguished one. It included William Cullen Bryant, who introduced him, Horace Greeley, David Dudley Field, and many other well-known men of the day.

Years later, Noah Brooks, a California newspaper man who became a Washington correspondent and friend of Lincoln, gave the report of a man who had been in the audience that night.

"When Lincoln rose to speak, I was greatly disappointed. He was tall, tall—oh, how tall—and so angular and awkward that I had, for an instant, a feeling of pity for so ungainly a man. His clothes were ill-fitting, badly wrinkled—as though they had been jammed carelessly into a small trunk. His bushy head with stiff black hair thrown back, was balanced on a long and lean headstalk, and when he raised his hands in an opening gesture I saw that they were very large. He began in a low tone of voice—as if he were used to speaking outdoors, and was afraid of speaking too loud. He said Mr. *Cheerman,* instead of Mr. *Chairman,* and employed many other words with an old-fashioned pronunciation. I said to myself:

" 'Old fellow, you won't do; it's all very well for the wild West, but this will never go down in New York.'

"But pretty soon he began to get into his subject; he straightened up, made regular and graceful gestures; his face lighted as with an inward fire; the whole man was transfigured. I forgot his clothes, his personal appearance, his individual peculiarities. Presently, forgetting myself, I was on my feet with the rest, yelling like a wild Indian, cheering this wonderful man. In the close parts of his arguments, you could hear the gentle sizzling of the gas burners. When he reached a climax the thunders of applause were terrific."

Lincoln closed the speech with these words: "Let us have faith that right makes might, and in that faith, let us, to the end, dare to do our duty as we understand it."

"It was a great speech," Brooks's informant said. "When I came out of the hall my face was glowing with excitement and my frame all a-quiver; a friend with eyes aglow, asked me what I thought of Abe Lincoln, the rail-splitter. I said, 'He's the greatest man since St. Paul.' "

The leading dailies published the speech in full next day and made editorial mention of it and of Lincoln. Lincoln had won New York, but at some point he had lost his watch. He inserted an advertisement in the New York *Herald:*

STOLEN, A WATCH WORTH A HUNDRED DOLLARS.
IF THE THIEF WILL RETURN IT, HE SHALL BE
INFORMED, GRATIS, WHERE HE MAY STEAL ONE
WORTH TWO OF IT, AND NO QUESTIONS ASKED.

Soon after the Cooper Union speech, Lincoln went on a speaking tour of New England. He delivered eleven speeches in two weeks and visited his son Robert who was attending the Phillips Academy in Exeter, New Hampshire.

In May the Illinois Republican party met in Decatur and committed the delegation to the Republican national convention to Lincoln. After the Decatur meeting an elderly Democrat from southern Illinois approached Abe on the street and said:

"So you're Abe Lincoln."

"Yes, that is my name."

"They say you're a self-made man."

"Well, yes; what there is of me is self-made."

"Well, all I've got to say," observed the man, after a careful survey of the Republican candidate, "is that it was a damned bad job."

Lincoln considered going to Chicago with the Illinois delegation, but finally declined.

"I am a little too much of a candidate to go," he said, "and not quite enough of a candidate to stay away; but on the whole I believe I will not go."

Three days before the meeting of the Republican national convention in Chicago, Lincoln was at home with his family in Springfield. Speaking of that quiet Sunday, Mrs. Lincoln said: "We had before us a New York illustrated weekly, in which a number of Presidential candidates were represented in a double-page group, Mr. Seward's portrait being conspicuous over all, as that of the coming man. Mr. Lincoln's picture was there, such as it was, and it couldn't have been made more dismal. Half-seriously I said to him, 'A look at that face is enough to put an end to hope.' "

William Henry Seward, genial and well-liked candidate of Thurlow Weed's New York State machine, was generally thought to have the nomination in his pocket—perhaps by acclamation. But the shrewd, tough Lincoln men argued, cajoled, fanned the flames of opposition to Seward, convinced wavering delegates with promises even though Lincoln had

After the slave states withdrew, a difficult task lay ahead. One contemporary artist drew Lincoln as the "Rail Splitter" at work repairing the Union.

sent a telegram saying: "Authorize no bargains and will be bound by none."

At the end of the second ballot Seward had 184½ votes against 181 for Lincoln. At the end of the third ballot he had almost won. Then, accompanied by the roar of ten thousand Illinoisans, delegates rose to change their votes. The final count was 354 votes out of 466 for Abraham Lincoln.

When the news of his nomination reached Springfield, Lincoln was standing in front of a store where he had gone to do an errand for his wife. After standing with the exulting crowd for a few moments, Lincoln said, "My friends, I am glad to receive your congratulations, and as there is a little woman down on Eighth Street who will be glad to hear the news, you must excuse me until I inform her."

Some of Mr. Lincoln's neighbors were as surprised by the news of his nomination for the Presidency as were people in distant states. One neighbor, an Englishman, could not contain his astonishment at the happening.

"What," he said, "*Abe Lincoln* nominated for President of the United States? Is it possible? A man that buys a ten-cent beefsteak for his breakfast and carries it home himself?"

The house on Eighth Street became a goal for job-seekers, political pilgrims, and "I-won't-believe-it-until-I-see-it" officials from all over the country. He transferred his law cases to his partner and used a room in the State House for conferences with the political advisors and other guests.

Sometimes there were meetings in the parlor of his home. Tad came into the room during one conference and said in a loud whisper, "Ma says come to supper." His father smiled and turned to his guests. "You have all heard, gentlemen, the announcement about the state of affairs in the dining room. If I am elected, it will never do to make this young man a member of my cabinet; it is plain he cannot be trusted with secrets of state."

During the long summer, while the campaign machinery

of the Republican party operated smoothly—Seward came to Springfield to promise a large New York State majority—Lincoln stayed home. He spoke briefly, and then mostly to ask to be allowed to say nothing.

He was about the only quiet man in the country. His party had come out flatly against the institution of slavery, and its program was to restrict it to the states where it already existed with the blessing of local constitutions and laws. The Douglas wing of the Democratic party, which had nominated its man for the Presidency, did not wish to deal with the morality of slavery. It proposed to sanction local sovereignty in new states and to abide by Supreme Court decisions as to what was constitutional.

The Buchanan wing of the Democratic party, which had nominated John C. Breckinridge for the Presidency, held that slavery was morally right; it was beneficial; all new states and territories should have it; and furthermore the island of Cuba should be immediately acquired as a source of supply.

Then there was the Constitutional Union party, which nominated John Bell for the Presidency and ignored the matter of slavery completely. The Democrats, led by the tireless Douglas, tried every approach to party unity and failed. And while the Democrats were in council chambers the Republican volunteers, the "Wide-Awakes," were campaigning in the streets from Maine to California.

Newton Bateman, Superintendent of Public Instruction for the State of Illinois, occasionally joined Lincoln for a private talk after one of the long days was over. One day in October, Lincoln called Bateman to his room in the State House and asked him to go over a survey of all the voters in Springfield, which listed how each citizen intended to cast his ballot.

"Let us look over this book," said Mr. Lincoln. "I wish particularly to see how the ministers of Springfield are going to vote." As they turned the pages, Mr. Lincoln asked if this one or that one were not a minister or an elder, or a member of this church or that.

When they had closed the book and Lincoln had looked at his notes, he turned to Bateman with inexpressible sadness.

"Here are twenty-three ministers of different denominations, and all of them are against me but three; and here are a great many prominent members of the churches, a very large majority of whom are against me. Mr. Bateman, I am not a Christian—God knows I would be one—but I have carefully read the Bible, and I do not so understand this book." Taking a copy of the New Testament out of his pocket, he continued.

"These men well know that I am for freedom in the territories, freedom everywhere as far as the Constitution and laws will permit, and that my opponents are for slavery. They know this; and yet, with this book in their hands, in the light of which human bondage cannot live a moment, they are going to vote against me. I do not understand it at all."

Mr. Lincoln paused, rose to his feet, and walked up and down the room with his head bowed. When he raised his face it was wet with tears.

"I know there is a God," he said, "and that He hates injustice and slavery. I see a storm coming, and I know that His hand is in it. If He has a place and work for me—and I think He has—I believe I am ready. I am nothing, but the truth is everything. I know I am right because I know liberty is right, for Christ teaches it and Christ is God. I have told them that 'a house divided against itself cannot stand' and Christ and reason say the same; and they will find it so. Douglas don't care whether slavery is voted up or voted down, but God cares, and humanity cares, and I care; and with God's help I shall not fail. I may not see the end, but it will come, and I will be vindicated; and these men will find that they have not read their Bibles aright."

In mid-October Lincoln received a letter from a very young lady in Westfield, New York.

Hon A B Lincoln

Dear Sir

My father has just home from the fair and brought home your picture and Mr. Hamlin's. I am a little girl only eleven years old, but want you should be President of the United States very much so I hope you wont think me very bold to write such a great man as you are. Have you any little girls about as large as I am if so give them my love and tell her to write to me if you cannot answer this letter. I have got 4 brother's and part of them will vote for you anyway and if you will let your whiskers grow I will try and get the rest of them to vote for you you would look a great deal better for your face is so thin. All the ladies like whiskers and they would tease their husband's to vote for you and then you would be President. My father is going to vote for you and if I was a man I would vote for you to but I will try and get every one to vote for you that I can I think that rail fence around your picture makes it look very pretty I have got a little baby sister she is nine weeks old and just as cunning as can be. When you direct your letter dir(e)ct to Grace Bedell Westfield Chatauque County New York

I must not write any more   answer this letter right off

Good bye
Grace Bedell

Lincoln answered promptly.

Miss. Grace Bedell   Springfield, Ills.

My dear little Miss.   Oct 19. 1860

Your very agreeable letter of the 15th, is received.

I regret the necessity of saying I have no daughters. I have three sons—one seventeen, one nine, and one seven, years of age. They, with their mother, constitute my whole family.

As to the whiskers, having never worn any, do you not think people would call it a piece of silly affection (*sic*) if I were to begin it now?

> Your very sincere well-wisher
> A. Lincoln.

On the sixth of November, 1860, Mr. Lincoln went as usual to his temporary office in the State House. Early in the day, crowds of friends and well-wishers began to descend upon him in such numbers that it was suggested that the doors be closed to keep them out. Lincoln said he'd never closed doors on his friends and did not intend to start now.

He had not planned to vote because his name headed the ticket and he didn't want to vote for himself. However, a friend fixed that by taking a ballot, cutting Mr. Lincoln's name off the top, and suggesting that Lincoln vote for the rest of the ticket.

The good news started about midnight—Pennsylvania for Lincoln, New York for Lincoln, Maine, New Hampshire, Ohio . . . seventeen free states and, causing one of the wildest cheers of all, New York City.

As soon as victory was certain Lincoln went home. "On my arrival," he said, "I went to my bedroom and found my wife fast asleep. I gently touched her shoulder and said, 'Mary'; she made no answer. I spoke again, a little louder, saying 'Mary, Mary, we are elected.'

"Well . . . I then went to bed, but before I went to sleep I selected every member of my Cabinet except one."

Lincoln told Noah Brooks a haunting incident that happened during the election excitement:

"It was just after my election in 1860, when the news had been coming in thick and fast all day, and there had been a great 'hurrah boys' so that I was well tired out, and went home to rest, throwing myself down on a lounge in my chamber. Opposite where I lay was a bureau and, looking in the glass, I saw myself reflected, nearly at full length; but my face, I noticed, had two separate and distinct images, the top of the nose of one being about three inches from the top of the other. I was a little bothered, perhaps startled, and got up and looked in the glass, but the illusion vanished. On lying down again I saw it a second time—plainer, if possible, than before; and then I noticed that one of the faces was a little paler, say five shades, than the other. I got up and the thing melted away and I went off, and in the excitement of the hour forgot all about it—nearly, but not quite, for the thing would come up once in a while and give me a little pang, as though something uncomfortable had happened. When I went home again that night I told my wife about it, and a few days afterward I tried the experiment again, when, sure enough, the thing came again; but I never succeeded in bringing the ghost back after that, though I tried industriously to show it to my wife, who was somewhat worried about it. She thought it was a 'sign' that I was to be elected to a second term of office, and that the paleness of one of the faces was an omen that I should not see life through the last term."

The final election returns showed that of the popular vote Lincoln had received 1,866,452—nearly half a million over Douglas, a million over Breckinridge, and a million and a quarter over Bell. Out of 303 electoral votes Lincoln had 180. It was a victory, but there were some aspects of the victory that gave the victors cause for thought. Lincoln had more popular votes than any one of his Democratic opponents, but he had a million less than the total Democratic vote. Out of 4,700,000 votes cast, Lincoln polled little more than a third. Fifteen states gave him no electoral votes at all, and in ten states not a single ballot was cast for him.

The slave states had threatened to secede if he were elected. They now set about it.

The Cabinet he formed in his mind the night of his election was remarkably close to the one that sat with him in the

Two months after his election, Lincoln appeared in Frank Leslie's paper as the "New Cabinet Maker."

White House following his inauguration. Lincoln had already said that he preferred "a Democrat that he knew to a Republican he didn't know," and he felt that party labels didn't matter. Five members of the Cabinet were Lincoln's political rivals. "They will eat you up," a friend warned. "They will eat each other up," Lincoln replied.

Salmon P. Chase, the handsome senator from Ohio, called upon Lincoln in Springfield to accept his appointment as Secretary of the Treasury. After Mr. Chase had left, a young man who had overheard the discussion went to Lincoln and complained about Mr. Chase.

"Don't like him?" said Mr. Lincoln. "Why, he is one of the most distinguished men in the country."

"I know that," the young man replied. "The trouble with him is, he thinks he's a bigger man than you are."

Lincoln laughed: "If you will find for me seven bigger men than I am, I'll put them all in the Cabinet."

Now came the bitter months of waiting. Lincoln was helpless to do anything about the rising tide of secession. He observed: "I would willingly take out of my life a period in years equal to the months which intervene between now and my inauguration. Because each hour adds to the difficulties I am called upon to meet, and the present administration does nothing to check the tendency towards dissolution."

To his friends in Billy Brown's store he said, "I wish I could have got down there before the horse was stole, but I reckon I can find the tracks when I do get there."

In answer to a direct question as to what he intended to do about the seceding states when he became Chief Executive, Lincoln told a story.

"Many years ago, when I was a young lawyer, and Illinois was little settled except on her southern border, I with other lawyers used to ride the circuit; journeying with the judge from county-seat to county-seat in quest of business. Once, after a long spell of pouring rain which had flooded the whole country, transforming small creeks into rivers, we were often stopped by these swollen streams which we with difficulty crossed. Still ahead of us was Fox River, larger than all the rest; and we could not help saying to each other, 'If these streams give us so much trouble, how shall we get over Fox River?' Darkness fell before we had reached that stream and we all stopped at a log tavern, had our horses put out, and resolved to pass the night. Here we were right glad to fall in with the Methodist Presiding Elder of the circuit, who rode out in all weather, knew all its ways, and could tell us about Fox River. So we all gathered around him and asked him if he knew anything about the crossing of Fox River. 'Oh, yes,' he replied, 'I know all about Fox River. I have crossed it often and understand it well; but I have one fixed rule with regard to Fox River. I never cross it till I reach it.' "

Five days before Christmas, South Carolina seceded from the Union. The new year came, and soon it would be time to leave Springfield for Washington, and there had been threats that he would be assassinated before he could arrive in the capital. The President-elect and his wife knew something of what life in Washington would be like, even though they did not agree with an article in the *Atlantic Monthly* which described it with a marked lack of restraint.

"If the beggars of Dublin, the cripples of Constantinople, and the lepers of Damascus should assemble in Baden-Baden during a Congress of Kings, then Baden-Baden would resemble Washington. Presidents, Senators, Honorables, Judges, Generals, Commodores, Governors, and Execs of all descriptions congregate here as thick as pickpockets at a horserace or women at a wedding in church. Add Ambassadors, Plenipotentiaries, Lords, Counts, Barons, Chevaliers, the great and small fry of the legations, Captains, Lieutenants, Claim Agents, Negroes, perpetual-motion men, Fire-Eaters, Irishmen, Plug Uglies, Hoosiers, Gamblers, Californians, Mexicans, Japanese, Indians, and Organ Grinders, together with females to match all varieties of males, and you have a vague notion of the people of Washington."

On February 4, 1861, representatives of South Carolina, Georgia, Florida, Alabama, Louisiana, and Mississippi met in Montgomery to form the Confederate States of America. Jefferson Davis was elected president.

Lincoln also heard of a scheme to take New York City out of the Union and establish it as a free city. "I reckon," he said, "that it will be some time before the front door sets up housekeeping on its own account. My opinion is that it is the duty of the President to run the machine as it is."

The Lincolns were to leave Springfield on February 11 and arrive in Washington twelve days later, with many stops and many public appearances.

Gifts of fine clothing had been showered upon them, and Lincoln said: "Well, Mother, if nothing else comes out of this scrape, we are going to get some new clothes, are we not?"

The day before he left Springfield, Lincoln went to his law office to get some books and papers he wanted to take with him. He asked that the signboard at the foot of the stairway be left the way it was.

"Let it hang there undisturbed. Give our clients to understand that the election of a President makes no difference in the firm." He paused and looked around. "If I live, I'm coming back sometime, and then we'll go right on practicing law as if nothing had ever happened."

A lady from New Salem, whom Ida Tarbell referred to as Aunt Sally Lowdy, came to see the President-elect at home one day when Billy Brown and many others were there.

Billy said, "Aunt Sally stood looking kind of scared seeing so many strangers and not knowing precisely what to do, when Mr. Lincoln spied her. Quick as a wink he said, 'Excuse me, gentlemen,' and he just rushed over to that old woman and shook hands with both of his'n and said, 'Now, Aunt Sally, this is real kind of you to come and see me.'

73

VOL. 4.

VANITY FAIR

NO. 99

Saturday,
NOVEMBER 16,
1861.

PUBLISHED EVERY SATURDAY, AT 100 NASSAU STREET, N.Y.

In November 1861, this drawing of Lincoln addressing England, France, and Spain appeared on the front cover of *Vanity Fair*. With the caption, "Boys, I reckon I wouldn't," it reflected American concern about the possibility of foreign intervention.

" 'Abe,' says Aunt Sally, all the old folks in Sangamon called him Abe. They knowed him as a boy, but don't you believe anybody ever did up here. No, sir. We said, 'Mr. Lincoln.' He was like one of us, but he wan't no man to be familiar with.

" 'Abe, they say down our way that they're going to kill you if they get you down to Washington, but I don't believe it. I just tell 'em you're too smart to let 'em git ahead of you that way. I thought I'd come and bring you a present, knit 'em myself'; and I'll be blamed if that old lady didn't pull out a great big pair of yarn socks and hand 'em to Mr. Lincoln."

On the way to Washington the Lincolns rode in an ordinary passenger car with the children. They made a stop in Westfield, New York, and the President-elect asked if little Miss Bedell, who had written him about the whiskers, was among those who had gathered to greet the Presidential party. She was brought to him, and Lincoln, lifting her in his arms and kissing her, introduced her to his new-grown beard.

When the train pulled into New York City the roaring of the crowds drowned out the blowing of the steam whistle of the train. Mrs. Lincoln looked out at the crowding mass of people. Then she opened her handbag and took out a comb. Turning to her husband she said:

"Abraham, I must fix you up a little for these city folks."

[10]

One of the pieces of baggage that the Lincolns took with them was a small satchel, containing the President-elect's inaugural address. At Harrisburg the satchel was given to

Robert Lincoln for safekeeping, but it somehow got lost and Lincoln was in despair. The satchel finally showed up, and Lincoln quickly removed the precious papers. The incident, he said, reminded him of a man who had deposited fifteen hundred dollars in a bank. The bank failed, and all the man got back was ten percent of his money. He deposited the hundred and fifty dollars in another bank that also failed, and again he was repaid ten percent. He gazed thoughtfully at the fifteen dollars and said, "Now, darn you, I have got you reduced to portable shape, so I'll put you in my pocket."

On the morning of March 4 Lincoln was up early in his rooms at Willard's Hotel, considering a note from Seward, who asked to be relieved of his promise to accept the post of Secretary of State. Lincoln answered Seward's letter instantly, begging him to reconsider. "I can't afford," he said to his secretary, "to let Seward take the first trick." Later he met President Buchanan, and they made their way to the platform erected on the east portico of the Capitol.

The President-elect was introduced by Senator Edward D. Baker of Oregon. Lincoln stood beside him, carrying the manuscript of his speech, a cane, and his tall silk hat. As he made ready to speak, he looked around for a place to put the hat. Stephen A. Douglas stepped quickly forward, took the hat, and returned to his seat. "If I can't be President," he said to a cousin of Mrs. Lincoln, "I can at least hold his hat."

The ugly situation grew uglier. All over the South, arsenals, forts, customhouses, and post offices were being seized by the secessionist states. Major Robert Anderson's garrison at Fort Sumter was being starved out, and almost every member of Lincoln's Cabinet thought he knew more about what ought to be done than the President.

A month after the inauguration, Mr. Seward wrote a long memorandum to Mr. Lincoln which contained, among other curious recommendations, the following: "I would demand explanations from France and Spain, energetically and at once . . . and if satisfactory explanations are not received from France and Spain, I would convene Congress and declare war against them."

The President answered this communication the same day he received it. He firmly pointed out his interpretation of the duties of the Chief Executive, and left no doubt in the Secretary of State's mind that he intended to be the Chief Executive. After he had finished the reply he murmured: "One war at a time, one war at a time."

On the twelfth of April the big guns of Charleston, S.C., opened fire on Fort Sumter. Thirty-four hours later, Major Anderson marched his men out of the smoking fort with colors flying and drums beating. On April 15 the President issued a call for 75,000 volunteers to enforce the laws of the Federal Government.

The sentiment of the North was unified by the bombardment of Sumter, but so was that of the South. Instead of a hundred voices in the land, there were now only two—the Union and the Confederacy. On April 17 Virginia declared for secession and notified the Confederacy to that effect. North Carolina, Tennessee, and Arkansas followed suit. From the White House Mr. Lincoln could now look across the placid Potomac to enemy-held territory. On April 18 a rumor reached the capital that a large Confederate force was marching on the city.

Resolving that Washington would be defended, several of the New England states began to rush soldiers to the capital. In Baltimore, while delegations of Marylanders protested about having their state befouled by the feet of soldiers marching against the South, the Sixth Massachusetts Regiment was attacked and four of its members were killed.

"We must have troops," Lincoln said, "and as they can neither crawl under Maryland nor fly over it they must come across it." He was warned that 75,000 citizens would oppose the troops. "I presume," said the Commander in Chief, "that you have room in Maryland for 75,000 graves."

Now the army of office-seekers increased. The White House

Before the War, England had depended on the Southern states for cotton. Many mills shut down when the supply was cut off. To some of the mill owners, the rights of the Negro were of little importance.

overflowed with them, and they all wanted to see the President "for just five minutes."

"I feel," Mr. Lincoln said, "like a man letting lodgings at one end of the house while the other end is on fire." With an incredible investment of time, he did see many of them, even to a man who was applying for the post of doorkeeper of the House.

"So you want to be doorkeeper to the House?" Mr. Lincoln asked.

"Yes, Mr. President."

"Well, have you ever been a doorkeeper? Have you ever had any experience in doorkeeping?"

"Well, no—no actual experience, Sir."

"Any theoretical experience? Any instructions in the duties and ethics of doorkeeping?"

"Um, no."

"Have you ever attended lectures on doorkeeping?"

"No, Sir."

"Have you ever read any textbooks on the subject? Have you ever conversed with anyone who has read such a book?"

"No, Sir. I'm afraid not, Sir."

"Well, then, my friend, don't you see you haven't a single qualification for this important post?" Mr. Lincoln said.

"Yes, I do," the applicant answered, and took his leave.

Day after day Mr. Lincoln was subjected to pressures exerted from all angles and all regions. One group called upon him with a candidate for commissioner to the Sandwich Islands. The President already had eight carefully screened applicants. He listened to the group, however, until they claimed that not only was their man qualified but he was also sick, and a stay in the agreeable climate of the islands would be of great benefit to him.

The President rose to his feet. "Gentlemen," he said, "I am sorry to say there are eight other candidates for that place, and they are all sicker than your man."

A group called upon the President to urge the appointment of some of their friends to a certain department. In refusing the request Mr. Lincoln said:

"Gentlemen, the conditions in that department put me in mind of the time a young friend and I tried to court the two daughters of a rather peppery widow living near our homes. The old lady kept a lot of hounds. We had not been in the house very long when one of the hounds came into the room and lay down by the fire. In a little while another one came to the door. He didn't get in, for the old lady gave him a kick, saying, 'Get out of here. There's too many dogs in here now.' We concluded to court some other girls."

"When I give away a place," Lincoln said, "I always make a hundred foes for one friend."

The President worked a sixteen- or eighteen-hour day, and he did not tolerate the slackness he saw around him. A woman who came to see him left with the following note signed by the President: "The lady bearer of this says she has two sons who want to work. Set them to it, if possible. Wanting to work is so rare a merit it should be encouraged."

In dealing with one job-seeker, Lincoln told a fable.

"Well, Sir, it seems like there was once an old king who was going hunting one day with all his courtiers. . . . He soon met a farmer on the road. The farmer told the king it was going to rain. But the king's astrologer didn't think so. About an hour later there came a cloudburst that proved the farmer to be right; so the king cut off the astrologer's head, and sent for the farmer and offered him the vacant office.

" 'It ain't me that knows when it's going to rain,' he said, 'It's my jackass. He lays his ears back.

" 'Then your jackass is hereby appointed court astrologer,' said the king. And afterwards he realized it was the biggest mistake of his life, because every jackass in the country wanted an office."

At one time the President had an attack of a mild form of

smallpox. When told what it was that was bothering him he said, "Good, now I have something I can give everyone."

One of Lincoln's old Illinois friends came job-hunting one day, and the President was eager to do something for him. The visitor was an honest man but wholly inexperienced in public affairs, and Mr. Lincoln was astonished when the man asked for high office—Superintendent of the Mint.

"Good gracious," he said, "why don't you ask to be Secretary of the Treasury and have done with it?"

Later he observed, "Well, now, I never thought he had anything more than average ability when we were young men together. But, then, I suppose he thought the same thing about me, and—here I am."

The President wasted no time making it known to the Cabinet that he intended to be President in fact as well as name. The Cabinet contained four former Democrats and three former Whigs, which had caused Thurlow Weed to inquire bitterly who had won the election. All the officers considered themselves the President's superior in one aspect or another. But as the weeks went by, the members of the Cabinet began to change their views. Two months after the beginning of the war, Seward wrote a letter to his wife which contained the statement, "The President is the best of all of us."

Edwin Stanton, who had taken such a dislike to Lincoln so many years before, was violently set against the President. He had served as President Buchanan's Attorney General and had recently become legal advisor to Simon Cameron, whom Lincoln had made Secretary of War.

Stanton was not a man to disguise his feelings. In a letter to a friend he wrote: "No one can imagine the deplorable condition of this city, and the hazard of the Government, who did not witness the weakness and panic of the Administration and the painful imbecility of Lincoln." Stanton frequently referred to the President as "a low, cunning clown." Stanton

81

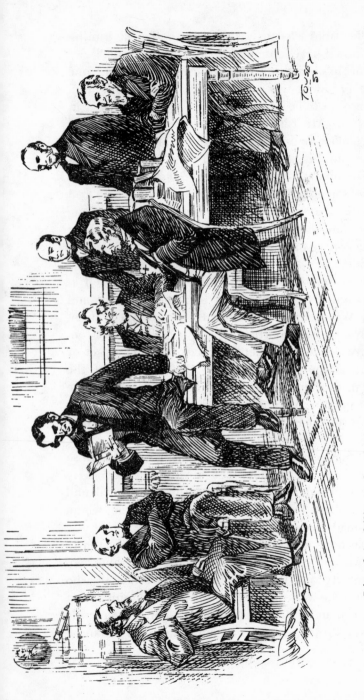

Lincoln's ability to laugh, even during the bleakest days of the war, often astonished the people who worked with him. At one meeting the cabinet sat dumfounded while he read aloud from a book of humor. After he finished he admonished the others: "Gentlemen, why don't you laugh? If I did not laugh I should die, and you need this medicine as much as I do."

has not been quoted on the subject of the immediate blockade of the Southern ports, called the one critical decision of the Commander in Chief, without which the war might well have been lost.

There was no telegraph apparatus in the White House. The news was brought to the President from the War Department, unless he went after it. He much preferred to go after it, and he began soon after the fall of Fort Sumter to run over to the department whenever anything important was going on. William B. Wilson, of Philadelphia, was in the military telegraph office of the War Department from the first of May, 1861, and in his recollections of Lincoln recalls an incident that occurred one day when Mr. Wilson had been sent to the White House to repeat an important message from an excited Governor.

"Mr. Lincoln considered it of sufficient importance," writes Wilson, "to return with me to the War Department for the purpose of having a wire-talk with the perturbed Governor. Calling one of his two younger boys to join him, we then started from the White House, between stately trees, along a gravel path which led to the rear of the old War Department building. It was a warm day, and Mr. Lincoln wore as part of his costume a faded gray linen duster which hung loosely around his long gaunt frame; his kindly face was beaming with good nature, and his ever-thoughtful brow was unruffled. We had barely reached the gravel walk before he stooped over, picked up a round, smooth pebble, and shooting it off with his thumb, challenged us to a game of 'followings' which we accepted. Each in turn tried to hit the outlying stone, which was constantly being projected onward by the President. The game was short but exciting; the cheerfulness of childhood, the ambition of young manhood, and the gravity of the statesman were all injected into it. The game was not won until the steps of the War Department were reached. Every inch of progression was toughly contested and when the President was declared victor, it was only by a handspan. He appeared to be as much pleased as if he had won a battle, and softened the defeat of the vanquished by attributing his success to greater height of person and longer reach of arm."

[11]

On Sunday, July 21, thirty miles southwest of Washington, the first major military engagement of the war was fought at Manassas Junction. During the day the news from the small stream called Bull Run went from bad to worse, and by midnight the President knew all he had to know about the magnitude of the disaster.

When a churchman announced, "The Lord is on our side," Lincoln commented: "I am not at all concerned about that, for we know that the Lord is always on the side of the right. But it is my constant anxiety and prayer that I and this nation should be on the Lord's side."

When the Union forces were routed at Bull Run, a large number of civilians were present, many of them carrying picnic lunches, who had gone out from Washington to witness the battle. Among that number were several congressmen. One of these was a tall, long-legged man, who wore a long-tailed coat and a high plug hat. When the retreat began, the congressman was in the lead of the entire crowd fleeing toward Washington. He outran all the rest, and was the first man to arrive in the city. No man ever made such good use of long legs. He went over ditches and gullies at a single leap, and cleared a six-foot fence with a foot to spare. As he went over the fence his plug hat blew off, but he did not pause.

Criticism of Lincoln's humor circulated widely in newspapers and magazines. Here he is caricaturized for telling jokes when there was urgent business to be done.

With his coattails flying in the wind, he continued straight ahead for Washington.

Many of those behind him were scared almost to death, but the flying congressman was such a comic figure that they had to laugh in spite of their terror.

Mr. Lincoln enjoyed the description of how the congressman led the race from Bull Run, and laughed at it heartily.

"I never knew but one fellow who could run like that," he said. "He was a young man out in Illinois who had been sparking a girl much against the wishes of her father. In fact, the old man took such a dislike to him that he threatened to shoot him if he ever caught him on the premises again.

"One evening the young man learned that the girl's father had gone to the city, and he ventured out to the house. He was sitting in the parlor with his arm around Betsey's waist, when he suddenly spied the old man coming around the corner of the house with a shotgun. Leaping through the window into the garden, he started down the path at the top of his speed like greased lightning. Just then a jackrabbit jumped up in the path in front of him. In about two leaps he overtook the rabbit. Giving it a kick that sent it high in the air, he yelled, 'Git out of the road, gosh dern you, and let somebody run that knows how. ' "

After the defeat at Bull Run, Stanton wrote, "The imbecility of this Administration culminated in that catastrophe; and irretrievable misfortune and national disgrace, never to be forgotten."

One immediate result of the battle was that Mr. Lincoln gave the command of the Army of the Potomac to General George B. McClellan. The brilliant, opinionated and—like most of the men who surrounded Lincoln—ambitious McClellan began to prepare the Army of the Potomac for combat. He prepared it and rehearsed it for weeks, clamoring for more men, horses, guns, and supplies, while the North was clamoring for action. The general was so insolent to the

President that Lincoln was advised to take some action about McClellan's attitude.

"Never mind," the President answered, "I'll hold Mc-Clellan's horse for him if he'll win some battles for me."

During these dark and indecisive days a gentleman from Kentucky called upon the President and asked what cheerful or reassuring news he could take back to his friends in Kentucky.

Mr. Lincoln replied: "That reminds me of a man who prided himself greatly on his game of chess, having rarely been beaten. He heard of a machine called 'The Automaton Chess Player' which was beating everyone who played against it. So he went to try his skill with the machine. He lost the first game, so with a second and with a third. Then, rising in astonishment from his seat, he walked around the machine and looked at it a few minutes. Then, stopping and pointing at it, he exclaimed, 'There is a man in there.'

"Tell my friends," said Mr. Lincoln, "there is a man in here."

Charles Sumner, the impeccable Bostonian, and the powerful Chairman of the Foreign Affairs Committee, was admitted to the President's bedroom one day and professed astonishment at finding Mr. Lincoln blacking his own shoes.

"Whose shoes," inquired the President, "did you expect to find me blacking, Mr. Sumner?"

In November the British mail packet, *Trent*, carrying Confederate commissioners James M. Mason and John Slidell to Great Britain, was stopped in international waters by a United States warship. Mason and Slidell were forcibly removed from the *Trent* and taken to Boston, where they were interned in Fort Warren. The act was enormously popular in the North. "We do not believe," wrote *The New York Times*, "that the American heart ever thrilled with more sincere delight."

Mr. Lincoln was not delighted, however; neither was

Senator Sumner of Massachusetts. They both believed that the British demand for the release of the two men was justified, and the envoys were subsequently released and sent on their way.

General McClellan was still preparing his army, and the Commander in Chief's patience was wearing thin. He referred once to the Army of the Potomac as "McClellan's bodyguard," and finally wrote a note to the effect that if General McClellan didn't plan to use the army for a while, he, Mr. Lincoln, would like to borrow it.

In December of the first bloody, bitter year of Lincoln's Presidency, Congress appointed a joint committee to inquire into the conduct of the war. There had been talk of corruption, and much of the talk was aimed at the Secretary of War, Simon Cameron. Thaddeus Stevens, the leading organizer of the Republican party in Pennsylvania, went to the President to object.

"You don't mean to say," Mr. Lincoln said, "that Cameron would steal?"

"No," Stevens replied, "I don't think he would steal a red-hot stove."

The remark was quoted to Cameron, who was enraged and demanded a retraction. Lincoln called the men together.

"Mr. Lincoln," Stevens said, "Cameron is very mad and made me promise to retract. I will now do so. I believe I told you that I didn't think he would steal a red-hot stove. I now take that back." Later the Secretary of War was persuaded to accept an ambassadorship. Republican leadership in Congress suggested that, as the President was divesting himself of his Secretary of War, it might be a good idea for him to make a clean sweep and select an entirely new cabinet. The President listened courteously to the deputation, and when they had completed their arguments he said:

"Gentlemen, your request for a change of the whole cabinet because I have made one change reminds me of a story I

One critic who considered Lincoln too idealistic pictured him as Don Quixote. General Benjamin Butler, as Sancho Panza, rides at his side.

once heard in Illinois of a farmer who was very much troubled by skunks. They annoyed his household at night, and his wife insisted that he should take measures to get rid of them. One moonlight night he loaded up his old shotgun and stationed himself in the yard to watch for the intruders, his wife remaining in the house anxiously awaiting results. After some time she heard the shotgun go off and in a few minutes the farmer entered the house.

" 'What luck had you?' she asked.

" 'I hid myself behind the woodpile,' said the old man, 'with the shotgun pointed towards the hen-roost, and before long there appeared, not one skunk, but *seven*. I took aim and blazed away, killed one, and he raised such a fearful smell that I concluded it was best to let the other six go.' "

To Simon Cameron's post Lincoln made one of his most controversial appointments. He selected Edwin Stanton, his tireless antagonist. Stanton shocked the President's friends by promptly accepting, with the statement, "I will make Abe Lincoln President of the United States." Along with his arrogance he had qualities that the Government needed desperately: he was honest; he had an enormous capacity for work; and he wouldn't put up with any nonsense from anybody. Lincoln's associates warned that Stanton would run away with the whole government.

"We may have to treat him," Lincoln observed, "as they are sometimes obliged to treat a Methodist minister I know out West. He gets wrought up to so high a pitch of excitement in his prayers and exhortations, that they have to put bricks in his pockets to keep him down. We may be obliged to serve Stanton the same way, but I guess we'll let him jump awhile first."

The impatient, irascible Stanton was determined to prosecute the war to the utmost, and he didn't intend to let the President interfere. Over the terrible task of waging war they slowly developed a remarkable admiration for each other.

Stanton took hold of his task with aggressive boldness. He was a friend of McClellan, but he let McClellan know what was expected. Stanton wrote Charles A. Dana, managing editor of Horace Greeley's *New York Tribune*: "This army has got to fight or run away; and while men are striving nobly in the west, the champagne and oysters on the Potomac must be stopped."

The President adopted the same stern view: "McClellan's tardiness," he said, "reminds me of a man in Illinois whose attorney was not sufficiently aggressive. The client knew a few law phrases, and finally, after waiting until his patience was exhausted by the nonaction of his counsel, he sprang to his feet and exclaimed: 'Why don't you go at him with a *Fi fa demurrer*, a *capias*, a *surrebutter*, or a *ne exeat* or something, and not stand there like a *nudum pactum*, or a *non est*.'"

One day a furious visitor approached Lincoln, saying that he had just left Secretary Stanton, who had called Lincoln a damned fool.

The President answered, "If Secretary Stanton called me a damned fool, then I probably am one, for the Secretary is usually right."

There were many interchanges of memoranda between the two. One such is preserved in the official Records of the War Department.

Dear Stanton: Appoint this man chaplain in the army. A. Lincoln.

Dear Mr. Lincoln: He is not a preacher. E. M. Stanton.

Dear Mr. Stanton: He is now. . . . A. Lincoln.

Dear Mr. Lincoln: But there is no vacancy. E. M. Stanton.

Dear Mr. Stanton: Appoint him Chaplain-at-large. A. Lincoln.

Dear Mr. Lincoln: There is no warrant for that. E. M. Stanton.

Dear Stanton: Appoint him anyhow. A. Lincoln.

Dear Mr. Lincoln: I will not. E. M. Stanton.

In the winter of 1862 citizens of the city of New York began to fear that their great harbor would be attacked by Confederate cruisers. Public meetings were held to consider the gravity of the situation. Finally a delegation of fifty of the wealthiest men in the city were chosen to go to Washington to ask the President to assign a gunboat to protect their property. They were introduced to the President, and the fact was stressed that their aggregate wealth totaled "hundreds of millions of dollars." Mr. Lincoln listened attentively.

"Gentlemen," he said in answer, "I am, by the Constitution, Commander-in-Chief of the Army and the Navy of the United States, and as a matter of law I can order anything to be done that is practicable to be done. I am in command of the gunboats and ships of war; but as a matter of fact I do not know exactly where they are. I presume they are actively engaged, and it is therefore impossible for me to furnish you with a gunboat. The credit of the government is at a very low ebb, gentlemen; greenbacks are not worth more than forty or fifty cents on the dollar; and in this condition of things, if I were worth half as much as you gentlemen are represented to be, and as badly frightened as you seem to be, I would build a gunboat and give it to the government."

The matter of greenbacks was a constant concern. An illustrated paper ran a cartoon showing Chase, Secretary of the Treasury, feeding gold to a United States goose that was laying greenbacks for eggs. Chase went to the President and denounced the lampoon as destructive of the government's credit, treasonable, demoralizing, and worthy of swift and terrible punishment.

"I myself," said Mr. Chase, "would give a hundred thousand dollars to make an example of its author."

Mr. Lincoln smiled at the Secretary of the Treasury. "From which end would you pay, Mr. Chase?"

One Cabinet meeting discussed the advisability of printing on a new issue of greenbacks an inscription similar to the "In

At the beginning of 1863, Union defeats were mounting. Cartoonist Thomas Nast saw little hope for the future.

God We Trust" that decorated the silver coins. When the President's opinion was asked, he said:

"If you want an inscription, I have one to suggest. It is from Peter and John: 'Silver and gold have I none, but such as I have I give thee.' "

The fall of Fort Henry and Fort Donelson in February supplied the North with the first good news of the war. For a while, the President felt a little better. Someone commented on the lack of pleasure and relaxation of his life. Mr. Lincoln agreed, and told a story about himself as a child.

"Once in a while my mother used to get some sorghum and some ginger and mix us up a batch of gingerbread. It wasn't often and it was our biggest treat. One day I smelled it and came into the kitchen to get my share while it was hot. I found that she had baked me three gingerbread men, and I took them out under a hickory tree to eat them. There was a family near us that was a little poorer than we were and their boy came along as I sat down.

" 'Abe,' he said, edging closer. 'Gimme a man.'

"I gave him one. He crammed it into his mouth in two bites and watched me while I bit off the legs of my first one.

" 'Abe,' he said, 'gimme the other one.'

"I wanted it, but I gave it to him anyway, and as it followed the first one down, I said: 'You seem to like gingerbread.'

" 'Abe,' he said, 'I don't s'pose there's anybody on this earth that likes gingerbread as much as I do—and I don't s'pose there's anybody gets less of it.' "

One of the President's few joys he found in the companionship of his younger sons Willie and Tad. He spent as much time with them as he could, and more than one distinguished visitor to the White House was amazed at the sight of Mr. Lincoln engaged in playground games with his sons in the corridors and reception rooms of the Executive Mansion. Presents for the President's sons came from everywhere, and Willie's favorite was a pony that he insisted upon riding every day around the White House grounds. The winter weather was treacherous, and Willie caught a severe cold accompanied by a high and increasing fever. On February 20, 1862, he died.

The funeral was held in the White House. Mrs. Elizabeth Keckley, a confidante of Mrs. Lincoln, described the event.

"The funeral was very touching. Of the entertainments in the East Room the boy had been a most life-giving variation. . . . He was his father's favorite. They were intimates —often seen hand in hand. And there sat the man, with a burden on the brain at which the world marvels—bent now with the load both at heart and brain—staggering under a blow like the taking from him of his child. His men of power sat around him—McClellan with a moist eye when he bowed to the prayer, as I could see from where I stood; and Chase and Seward, with their austere features at work; and senators, ambassadors and soldiers, all struggling with their tears— great hearts sorrowing with the President as a stricken man and a brother. That God may give him strength for all his burdens is, I am sure, the prayer of a nation."

[12]

In April McClellan finally moved his Army of the Potomac against the enemy. Striking south by way of the peninsula between the James and the York rivers, he prepared to attack Yorktown. The Confederates allowed McClellan to complete his careful, lengthy preparations for the assault, and evacuated the fortress without firing a shot. McClellan then moved in a complicated series of forays, which only succeeded in giving Lincoln the idea that he was trying to win the war by tactics rather than by fighting.

McClellan's dispatches to the White House consisted of constant demands for more men, guns, and horses, and many instructions about running the country. When Mr. Lincoln was asked how he responded to these instructions, he said:

"I answered nothing, but it made me think of the Irishman whose horse kicked up and got his foot caught in the stirrup. 'Arrah,' said the Irishman, 'if you're going to get on, I'm going to get off.' "

As the weeks of marching and countermarching went on, the Commander in Chief grew impatient.

"It seems to me," Mr. Lincoln said one day, "that McClellan has been wandering around and has sort of got lost. He's been hollering for help ever since he went south. Wants somebody to come to his deliverance and get him out of the place he's got into.

"He reminds me of the story of a man out in Illinois who, in company with a number of friends, visited the State Penitentiary. They wandered all through the institution and saw everything, but just about the time to depart, this particular man became separated from his friends and couldn't find his way out.

"He roamed up and down one corridor after another, becoming more desperate all the time, when at last, he came across a convict who was looking out from between the bars of his cell-door. Our man hurried up to the prisoner and asked:

" 'Say, how do you get out of this place?' "

McClellan grew angry at requests that he give more detailed reports, and began to concentrate on trivia. One dispatch read as follows:

President Abraham Lincoln, Washington, D.C.:
We have just captured six cows. What shall we do with them?
George B. McClellan

The President answered immediately:

Relaxing from the pressures of his office, Lincoln spent whatever time he could playing with his young sons. The boys shocked White House visitors by breaking into conferences or sitting in their father's lap during dinner. This picture of the President and his youngest son, "Tad," is copied from the famous photograph by Mathew Brady.

George B. McClellan, Army of the Potomac:
As to the six cows captured—milk them.

A. Lincoln

After a series of bloody and inconclusive battles, McClellan beat a masterly retreat before inferior forces commanded by Robert E. Lee.

The President was asked to estimate the Confederate force in the field, and he put it at over a million men. He said he arrived at the estimate because whenever one of his generals lost an engagement he claimed he was outnumbered four to one.

A major general accused Stanton of favoritism. The accusation infuriated Stanton, who wrote a violent reply. He took the letter to Lincoln and read it aloud. The President frequently interrupted him by saying, "That's right, Stanton, give it to him, that's just what he deserves, good for you."

When Stanton had finished, he folded the letter to put it in an envelope.

"What are you going to do with it now?" Lincoln asked.

"Why, send it, of course."

"Don't do it, Stanton," Lincoln said.

"But you just said it was exactly what he deserved," Stanton replied.

"Yes," said Lincoln, "I believe he does deserve it, but you don't want to send such a letter as that. Put it in the fire. That's what I do when I get angry. It's a good letter, and you have had a good time writing it and you feel better, don't you? It has done you good and answered its purpose. Now burn it."

In August the Union forces were defeated again at Bull Run, and General Lee moved across the Potomac to invade Maryland and Pennsylvania. General McClellan engaged Lee's army at Antietam Creek in September, and in the bloodiest battle of the war the two armies fought each other to exhaustion. McClellan was under the impression that he was outnumbered two to one, whereas in fact his troops outnumbered the enemy two to one. McClellan rested while Lee withdrew and regrouped.

"I was more discouraged after Antietam than at any other period," Stanton told Marcus Ward, "and the future seemed more obscure to me than at any previous time. But I kept on my daily work, and on the 22nd of September, 1862, I had a sudden and peremptory call to a meeting at the White House.

"I had to be constantly at my post, and it was only on rare and important occasions that I was called to such meetings. I went immediately to the White House, entered the room, and found the historic War Cabinet of Abraham Lincoln assembled, every member being present. The President hardly noticed me as I came. He was reading a book of some kind, which seemed to amuse him. It was a little book. He finally turned to us and said:

" 'Gentlemen, did you ever read anything from Artemus Ward? Let me read you a chapter that is very funny,'

"Not a member of the Cabinet smiled; as for myself, I was angry and looked to see what the President meant.

"It seemed to me like buffoonery. He, however, concluded to read us a chapter of Artemus Ward, which he did with great deliberation. Having finished, he laughed heartily, without a single member of the Cabinet joining in the laughter."

What the President read was the following piece called "High-Handed Outrage at Utica."

"In the fall of 1856, I showed my show in Utiky, a trooly grate sitty in the State of New York.

"The people gave me a cordyal recepshun. The press was loud in her prases.

"1 day as I was givin a descripshun of my Beests and Snaiks

99

in my usual flowry stile what was my skorn & disgust to see a big burly feller walk up to the cage containin' my wax figgers of the Lord's Last Supper, and cease Judas Iscarrot by the feet and drag him out on the ground. He then commenced fur to pound him as hard as he cood.

" 'What under the sun are you abowt?' cried I.

"Sez he, 'what did you bring this pussylanermus cuss here fur?' & he hit the wax figger another tremenjis blow on the hed.

"Sez I, 'You egrejus ass, that air's a wax figger—a representashun of the false 'Postle.'

"Sez he, 'That's all very well fur you to say, but I tell you, old man, that Judas Iscarrot can't show himself in Utiky with impunerty by a darn site,' with which observashun he kaved in Judassis hed. The young man belonged to 1 of the first famerlies in Utiky. I sood him, and the Joory brawt in a verdick of Arson in the 3d degree."

"I was considering," Stanton continued, "whether I should rise and leave the meeting abruptly, when he threw the book aside, heaved a long sigh, and said:

" 'Gentlemen, why don't you laugh? With the fearful strain that is upon me night and day, if I did not laugh I should die, and you need this medicine as much as I do.'

"He then put his hand in his tall hat that sat upon the table and pulled out a little paper. Turning to the members of the Cabinet he said:

" 'Gentlemen, I have called you here upon very important business. I have prepared a piece of paper of much significance. I have made up my mind that this paper is to issue; that the time has come when it should issue; that the people are ready for it to issue. It is due to my Cabinet that you should be the first to hear and know of it, and if any of you have any suggestions to make as to the form of this paper or its composition, I shall be glad to hear them. But the paper is to issue.'

"To my astonishment," Stanton went on, "he read the

United States Military Telegraph.

...

Received Oct 25 1862.

From Washington 4 50 Pm

To Maj' Gen McClellan

I have just read your despatch about sore tongued and fatigued horses. Will you pardon me for asking what the horses of your army have done since the battle of Antietam that fatigues anything?—

A Lincoln

A humorous reprimand. This note to General McClellan reflected the President's disgust with the General's progress.

Emancipation Proclamation of that date, which was to take effect the first of January following, containing the vital provision that on January 1st, 1863, all persons held as slaves within any state or designated part of a state, the people whereof shall be in rebellion against the United States, shall be then, henceforward and forever free."

Stanton said he approached the President with great enthusiasm, saying, "Mr. President, if the reading of chapters of Artemus Ward is a prelude to such a deed as this, the book should be filed among the archives of the nation and the author should be canonized. Henceforth, I see light and the country saved. And all said 'Amen.' "

Salmon P. Chase, in reporting the same meeting, said, ". . . President mentioned that Artemus Ward had sent him his book. Proposed to read a chapter which he thought very funny. Read it and seemed to enjoy it very much; the heads also, except Stanton of course."

In describing the reading of the text of the proclamation, Lincoln said when he finished there was a dead silence.

"Presently Mr. Chase spoke. He said he liked all but so and so, instancing a clause; then someone else made an objection, and then another, until all had said something."

"Gentlemen," said the President, "you remind me of the story about a man who had been away from home, and when he was coming back he was met by one of his farm hands, who greeted him after this fashion. 'Master, the little pigs are dead, and the old sow's dead too, but I didn't like to tell you all at once.' "

The members of Lincoln's Cabinet were restless men. Perhaps especially Mr. Chase. One of Lincoln's friends warned him that Mr. Chase was quietly working to secure the nomination for the Presidency. The friend stated that the President ought to tell Mr. Chase either to give up his notions of running for President or get out of the Cabinet. The advice reminded Lincoln of a story.

"My cousin and I," he said, "were once plowing corn. I was driving the horse and he holding the plow. The horse was lazy, but on one occasion he rushed across the field so that I, with my long legs, could scarcely keep up with him. On reaching the end of the furrow, I found an enormous chin-fly fastened on upon his neck, and knocked the fly off. My cousin asked me what I did that for. I told him I didn't want the old horse bitten that way. 'Why,' my cousin said, 'that's all that made him go.' Now, if Mr. Chase has a presidential chin-fly biting him, I'm not going to knock it off, if it will only make his department go."

On October 24 the President had sent a letter to General McClellan that left no doubt as to his feeling about the progress of the war.

"I have just read your dispatch about sore-tongued and fatigued horses. Will you pardon me for asking what the horses of your army have done since the battle of Antietam that would fatigue anything? A. Lincoln."

The most important immediate effect of the Emancipation Proclamation was not at home, however, but abroad. England, starving for cotton, had frequently expressed her interest in a negotiated peace between the North and the South, and the establishment of two separate countries. Napoleon III, Emperor of the French, had suggested to England and Russia that the three countries join in an attempt to mediate between the American belligerents. Both Russia and England refused. The motive of Emperor Alexander has been ascribed to his hatred of slavery, his own most famous action having been the liberation of the Russian serfs—one of a series of reforms for which he was eventually assassinated. The motives of the British ministry seem more complex, but it has been suggested that the pro-Northern factions of the British cabinet simply convinced their colleagues that the North was going to win.

In December, 1862, under the command of General

Ambrose E. Burnside, the Army of the Potomac again advanced on Richmond. Burnside led his "three grand divisions" against Lee at Fredericksburg. For two days he sent wave after wave of his crack troops against an impregnable position, and then Burnside withdrew, having slaughtered thirteen thousand of his men.

Among the throng who called daily upon the President was a man who requested that the President issue him a pass to go to Richmond.

"Well," said the President, "I would be happy to oblige, sir, but my passes are not respected. In the last year and a half I have given passes to two hundred and fifty thousand men to go to Richmond, and not one has got there yet."

But in the West the Army of the Tennessee, under the command of a general named Ulysses S. Grant, had been fighting and winning. Grant was careless in his dress and abrupt in his manners. Lincoln was told he drank to excess. "Find out what he drinks," the President said, "and send a barrel of it to my other generals."

When the President heard of a Union brigadier general and a number of horses being captured in a Confederate raid, he said he was sorry to hear about the horses.

"Sorry about the *horses,* Mr. President?" Stanton exclaimed.

"Yes," replied Mr. Lincoln, "I can make a brigadier general in five minutes, but it is not easy to replace a hundred and ten horses."

The Reverend Byron Sunderland, Chaplain of the Senate, called on the President in December because he had heard a rumor that Mr. Lincoln was going to withdraw the Emancipation Proclamation.

"We were ushered into the cabinet room," said Dr. Sunderland. "It was very dim, but one gas-jet was burning. As we entered, Mr. Lincoln was standing at the farther end of a long table that filled the middle of the room. As I stood by

In March of 1864, Lincoln named a new general to clean up where the others had failed. Here he considers his new appointment, General Ulysses S. Grant.

the door, I am so very short that I had to look up to see the President. Mr. Robbins introduced me, and I began at once by saying: 'I have come, Mr. President, to anticipate the new year with my respect, and if I may, to say a word about the serious condition of this country.'

" 'Go ahead, Doctor,' replied the President; 'every little helps.' But I was much too much in earnest to laugh at his sally at my smallness. 'Mr. President,' I continued, 'they say that you are not going to keep your promise to give us an Emancipation Proclamation; that it is your intention to withdraw it.

" 'Well, Doctor,' said Mr. Lincoln, 'you know Peter was going to do it, but when the time came he didn't.'

" 'Mr. President,' I continued, 'I have been studying Peter. He did not deny his Master until after his Master rebuked him in the presence of the enemy. You have a master too, Mr. Lincoln, the American people. Don't deny your master until he has rebuked you before all the world.'

"My earnestness seemed to interest the President, and his whole tone changed immediately. 'Sit down, Doctor Sunderland,' he said; 'let us talk.'

"We seated ourselves in the room, and for a moment the President was silent, his elbow resting on the table, his big gnarled hands closed over his forehead. Then, looking up gravely at me, he began to speak:

" 'Doctor, if it had been left to you and me, there would have been no cause for this war; but it was not left to us. God has allowed men to make slaves of their fellows. He permits this war. He has before Him a strange spectacle. We, on our side, are praying Him to give us victory, because we believe we are right; but those on the other side pray Him, too, for victory, believing they are right. What must He think of us? And what is coming from the struggle? What will be the effect of it all on the whites and on the Negroes?' And then suddenly a ripple of amusement broke the solemn tone of his voice. 'As for the Negroes, Doctor, and what is going to become of them; I told Ben Wade the other day that it made me think of a story I read in one of my first books, *Aesop's Fables*. It was an old edition and had curious, rough woodcuts, one of which showed four white men scrubbing a Negro in a potash kettle filled with cold water. The text explained that the men thought that by scrubbing the Negro they could make him white. Just about the time they thought they were succeeding he took cold and died. Now, I am afraid that by the time we get through with this war the Negro will take cold and die.'

"The laugh had hardly died away before he resumed his grave tone, and for half an hour discussed the question of emancipation. He stated it in every light, putting his points so clearly that every statement was an argument. He showed the fullest appreciation for every side. It was like a talk of one of the old prophets. And though he did not tell me at the end whether the Proclamation would be issued or not, I went home comforted and uplifted, and I believed in Abraham Lincoln from that day."

[13]

During the war the Armies of the North were weakened and demoralized by great numbers of desertions and examples of cowardice in the face of the enemy. All death penalties of courts-martial had to be forwarded to the Commander in Chief for approval, and Edward Bates, Lincoln's Attorney General, took grave and constant exception to the number of times the President pardoned convicted soldiers. Bates claimed that this lack of sternness was a marked defect in

Lincoln's character, and made him unfit to be trusted with pardoning power.

Stanton had to endure most of the complaints on the part of the military establishment, which claimed, with some justification, that the President's well-known attitude encouraged desertion and insubordination.

The Secretary of War's temper and lack of patience were well known, and some people tried to bypass him and get directly to the President. To one such man, the President said: "I cannot interfere. I must not offend Secretary Stanton."

"That cannot be," the petitioner said. "I have preferred to make my application to the President, who listens patiently, which Secretary Stanton will not always do."

"Perhaps," said Mr. Lincoln, "there is that difference between the Secretary and myself, and it recalls a story told to me by Swett: A man had a small bull terrier that could whip all the dogs of the neighborhood. The owner of a large dog that had been whipped by the terrier asked the owner of the terrier how it happened that his dog whipped every dog he encountered.

" 'That,' said the owner of the terrier, 'is no mystery to me; your dogs and other dogs get half way through a fight before they are really mad; my dog is always mad.' "

One of the President's secretaries reported that, after a set-to with Stanton about pardons, Mr. Lincoln said:

"I had a pretty hard time with the Secretary of War. Stanton makes a bully good Secretary. The only trouble with him is that he has no more philoprogenitiveness than an alligator who lays a pile of eggs in the burning sand and thinks he's done his whole duty by his family."

Judge Joseph Holt, the Judge Advocate General of the Army, laid a case before the President and explained it. Mr. Lincoln said:

"Well, I will keep this a few days until I have more time to read the testimony."

Allow the bearer, S. S. Bradford, to pass by any route to
his home in Culpeper Co.
Va, and there to remain
as long as he does not mis-
behave,

A. Lincoln

Dec. 21, 1864.

A pass for a man to return safely to his home in Virginia—one of
many special requests granted by the President.

The judge explained the next case. Mr. Lincoln replied:

"I must put this by until I can settle in my mind whether this soldier can better serve the country dead than living."

To the third he answered, "The general commanding the brigade will be here in a few days to consult with Stanton and myself about military matters; I will wait until then, and talk the matter over with him."

The President found it especially hard to deny a direct appeal from friends and relatives of the soldier involved. This aspect of the President's thinking was well known to Judge Holt, who came one day with a case that he thought even Lincoln would have to approve. It concerned a soldier who had thrown down his gun in the middle of a battle and hidden behind a stump until the shooting was over. When tried for his cowardice, there was no defense. Testimony at the court-martial revealed that he had no father or mother living, no wife, no children, and, as he constantly stole from his comrades, no friends, either.

"Here," said Judge Holt, "is a case which comes exactly within your requirements. He does not deny his guilt, he will serve the country better dead than living, as he has no relations to mourn for him, and he is not fit to be in the ranks of patriots."

The President deliberated for a while, then he turned to Holt.

"Well, after all, Judge, I think I'll have to put this with my 'leg cases.' "

"Leg cases?" asked Judge Holt, "what do you mean by 'leg cases,' sir?"

"Why, Judge," replied Mr. Lincoln, "do you see those papers crowded into those pigeonholes? They are cases that you call by that long name, 'cowardice in the face of the enemy,' but I call them for short my 'leg cases.' I put it to you, and I leave for you to decide for yourself: If Almighty God gives a man a cowardly pair of legs, how can he help their running away with him?"

Congressman John B. Alley, while passing through the crowded anteroom of the President's office, noticed an old man sitting in the corner, crying bitterly. The old man had a familiar story: his son had been condemned to be shot, and his congressman was so convinced of the boy's guilt that he refused to intervene. Mr. Alley took the man into the President's office and had him tell the story again. Mr. Lincoln was saddened and he replied:

"I am sorry to say I can do nothing for you. Listen to this telegram received yesterday from General Butler: 'President Lincoln. I pray you not to interfere with the court-martial of the army. You will destroy all discipline among our soldiers.'"

The visitor's hope drained away. The President looked at his stricken face, then he explained:

"By jingo, Butler, or no Butler, here goes." He wrote out a note and handed it to the old man. The note read, "Job Smith is not to be shot until further orders from me. A. Lincoln."

The old man looked at it unbelievingly. "I thought it was going to be a pardon," he said, "but you might decide to have him shot next week."

Mr. Lincoln smiled. "My friend," he said, "I see you are not very well acquainted with me. If your son never looks upon death till further orders come from me to shoot him, he will live to be a great deal older than Methuselah."

A friend came to the President with a request for mercy in the case of a Kentucky boy who had been enticed into the Confederate Army, had deserted, and made his way back home, where he had been arrested as a spy and sentenced to be hanged. Mr. Lincoln examined the evidence carefully and commented: "If a man had more than one life, I think a little hanging would not hurt this one, but as a man has only one life I think I'll pardon him."

Lincoln's old supporter Thaddeus Stevens, who criticized him frequently for actions like this, brought a mother from his own state of Pennsylvania to the White House. The lady's son was condemned to die for sleeping at his post. Lincoln listened carefully to the story and then turned to Stevens, knowing well how many of Stevens' constituents were interested in the case.

"Now, Thad," asked the President, "what would you do in this case, if you had happened to be President?"

Stevens did not enjoy the corner into which Mr. Lincoln had pushed him, but he replied that in view of the extenuating circumstances he would certainly pardon him.

Lincoln reached for a piece of paper and wrote on it. "Here, Madam," he said, "is your son's pardon."

Mr. Stevens escorted the grateful woman to the outer door of the White House, where she turned to him and exclaimed:

"I knew it was a lie. I knew it was a lie."

"What do you mean?" Mr. Stevens asked.

"When I left home yesterday," the woman said, "my neighbors told me that I would find that Mr. Lincoln was an ugly man. It was a lie; he is the handsomest man I ever saw in my life."

An important politician came to the President in a towering rage on one occasion, and when he had left, one of Mr. Lincoln's friends observed: "I suppose you found it necessary to make large concessions to him, as he appeared to be perfectly satisfied."

"Oh, no," said the President. "I did not concede anything. You have heard how the Illinois farmer got rid of a big log that was too big to haul out, too knotty to split, and too wet and soggy to burn?

" 'Well, now,' said he, in response to the inquiries of his neighbors one Sunday, as to how he got rid of it, 'well boys, if you won't divulge the secret, I'll tell you how I got rid of it—I ploughed around it.'

"Now," Mr. Lincoln concluded, "don't tell anybody, but that's the way I got rid of the Governor. I ploughed all

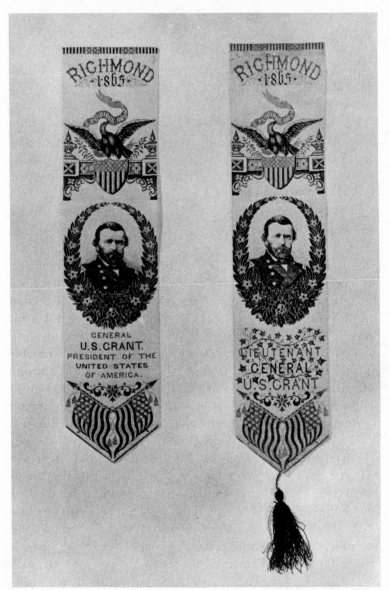

Two commemorative ribbons honor the North's top military hero at his best. General Ulysses S. Grant actually was a sloppy dresser and a heavy drinker. But, unlike his predecessors, he distinguished himself by fighting and winning.

around him, but it took me three mortal hours to do it, and I was afraid every minute he'd see what I was at."

In March of 1863 the President signed the first draft bill in the nation's history, and the voices of antagonism to his administration screamed louder than ever. When a call for extra troops came, citizens of Chicago were outraged. They had already sent twenty-two thousand men. Joseph Medill, editor of the *Chicago Tribune*, called on the President with a delegation to see about reducing the quota. Medill wrote this account of the meeting:

"On reaching Washington we went to Stanton with our statement. He refused entirely to give us support. We went on to Lincoln himself.

" 'I cannot do it,' the President said, 'but I will go with you to the War Department, and Stanton and I will hear both sides.'

"So we went to the War Department together. The argument went on for some time.

"I shall never forget how suddenly he lifted his head and turned on us with a black and frowning face. 'Gentlemen,' he said, in a voice full of bitterness, 'after Boston, Chicago has been the chief instrument in bringing war to this country. You called for war until we had it. You called for emancipation, and I have given it to you. Whatever you have asked, you have had. Now you come here begging to be let off from the call for men, which I have made to carry out the war which you have demanded.

" 'Go home and raise your six thousand extra men. And you, Medill, you are acting like a coward. You and your *Tribune* had more influence than any other paper in the Northwest in making this war.'

"I couldn't say anything. It was the first time I was ever whipped, and I didn't have an answer.

"We did raise those men—six thousand of them. But there probably was crepe on every door in Chicago, for every

114

family had lost a son or a husband. It was especially hard for the mothers."

In answering another objection to new drafts, Lincoln said that he would continue to call for extra men if the country required it, and quoted the response of a Western provost marshal who had been asked if the Confederate States enforced conscription. The provost marshal said: "Hell, stranger, I should think they do. They take every man who hasn't been dead for more than two days."

In April of 1863 Mr. and Mrs. Lincoln and Tad spent several days inspecting the Army of the Potomac with its new commander, "Fighting Joe" Hooker.

"April 8th," wrote Noah Brooks, "was the review of the Fifth Corps, under Meade; the Second, under Couch; the Third under Sickles, and the Sixth under Sedgwick. It was reckoned that these four corps numbered some 60,000 men, and it was a splendid sight to witness their grand martial array as they wound over hills and rolling ground, coming from miles away, their arms shining in the distance, and their bayonets bristling like a forest on the horizon as they marched away. The President expressed himself as being delighted with the appearance of the soldiery, and he was much impressed by the parade. It was noticeable that the President merely touched his hat in return salute to the officers, but uncovered to the men in the ranks. After a few days the weather grew warm and bright and the President became more cheerful, even jocular. I remarked this one evening as we sat at Hooker's headquarters.

" 'It is a great relief to get away from Washington and the politicians,' Lincoln said, 'but nothing touches the tired spot.' "

Before the new grass could cover the graves of the Union dead at Fredericksburg, Hooker marched his soldiers south again toward Richmond and crossed the Rappahannock.

The Army of Northern Virginia, commanded by Robert

Political campaign cartoon, 1864. McClellan avocated calling a halt to the war and restoring the Union. Lincoln wanted Grant to fight through to a clear-cut vic-

E. Lee and Stonewall Jackson, and half the size of the Army of the Potomac, waited at Chancellorsville. Four days later Hooker's corps, slashed and pounded to bloody fragments, retreated across the river counting seventeen thousand casualties.

Stunned by the news, the President murmured: "What will the country say? Oh, what will the country say?"

The country let him know in an avalanche of mail— measureless denunciation and pitiful pleas for an end to the long murder.

To a man who criticized his Administration most vociferously, Lincoln told the following story:

"A traveler on the frontier found himself, as night came on, in a wild region. A terrible thunderstorm added to his trouble. He floundered along until his horse gave out, and then he had to dismount to lead him. Occasional flashes of lightning afforded the only clue to the path, and the crashes of thunder were frightful. One bolt which seemed to crush the earth beneath him, made him stagger and brought him to his knees. Being by no means a praying man, his petition was short and to the point: 'Oh, Lord, if it's all the same to you, give us a little more light and a little less noise.' "

Lincoln once said about a critic, "He's the biggest liar in Washington. He reminds me of an old fisherman who had the reputation for stretching the truth. He got a pair of scales and insisted on weighing every fish he caught in front of witnesses. One day a doctor borrowed his scales to weigh a new baby. The baby weighed forty-seven pounds."

Some of the attacks upon the President were so vicious and unfounded that Lincoln was urged to reply to set the record straight by stating the facts.

He always refused. "If I were to try to read, much less answer, all the attacks made upon me, this shop might just as well be closed for any other business. I do the very best I know how—the very best I can; and I mean to keep on doing so until the end. If the end brings me out right, what is said against me won't amount to anything. If the end brings me out wrong, ten thousand angels swearing I was right wouldn't make any difference."

But there was no possible change of course. General Lee was reinforcing and reorganizing his army, and it was evident that he meant to move north through the Shenandoah Valley. The Commander in Chief was paying closer and closer attention to the movements of the Army of the Potomac. On June 5 he warned General Hooker not to run the risk of becoming entangled on the Rappahannock "like an ox jumped half over a fence, and liable to be torn by dogs, front and rear, without a fair chance to gore one way or kick the other." A few days later he wrote another dispatch. "If the head of Lee's army is at Martinsburg and the tail of it on the Plank road between Fredericksburg and Chancellorsville, the animal must be very slim somewhere. Could you not break him?"

Toward the end of June General Hooker resigned his command and was replaced by General George G. Meade. In the first week of July General Lee sent his army against Meade at Gettysburg. Lincoln, the American people, and the world waited through three days of savage battle until Lee withdrew his broken army. The total casualties of the rendezvous in the quiet Pennsylvania countryside numbered almost fifty thousand Americans.

Lincoln ordered Meade to move against Lee at once, certain that he could crush the Army of Northern Virginia forever, and possibly end the war. Meade delayed, however, and Lee was permitted to withdraw with his army still a fighting unit.

When the news of Grant's conquest of Vicksburg arrived it seemed as if the tide had turned at last.

A dossier that came to the President's desk soon after, involved the case of Billy Pomeroy, a Mississippi River pilot who had applied for command of a new armored gunboat. Billy's request was enthusiastically endorsed by his superior officers, but he still had to make an official appearance before a board of review.

"Who succeeded Cromwell?" asked the chairman of the committee for a starter.

"Tom Watson," Billy replied.

"Are you drunk," asked the chairman, "to trifle with the board in this fashion?"

"Well, I guess I ought to know what I'm talking about," Billy said, "old Sam Cromwell was captain of the *Lady Gay* until he died, and Tom Watson succeeded him."

"Our question does not refer to steamboat captains," the chairman explained, "but to the Lord Protector of England."

"Oh," said Billy, "I don't know, and I don't care a damn. I'm not applying for his place."

The board marked Billy's application with the words: "Not recommended—ignorant and insolent," but Billy's sponsors arranged for the application to reach the Commander in Chief.

Mr. Lincoln returned the file to the board with the following note:

"As nearly as anyone can guess, this seems to be a triangular contest between Charles Stuart, Oliver Cromwell, and Billy Pomeroy. It is generally believed here that both Charles and Oliver are dead. If, upon investigation, the board finds such to be the fact, give the job to Billy."

The whole Mississippi was open to Union gunboats, and the Confederacy was divided. But the growing hopes of the North were shattered at Chickamauga Creek on September 20, where a rout was averted by the stand of General George H. Thomas. A month later, reinforced by troops under the command of General Grant and General William T. Sher-

McCLELLEN.

THE GUNBOAT CANDIDATE
AT THE BATTLE OF MALVERN HILL.

Republicans attacked McClellan for his military failures. Here he
is shown sitting on the bowsprit of a gunboat, watching a battle
from afar.

man, the Union Army got a measure of revenge and re-opened supply lines. By the end of November the Confederate Army was in full retreat toward Georgia.

During November the President had gone to Gettysburg to dedicate the National Cemetery. The morning of his departure was a busy one, and his aides were concerned that he would not be on time for the scheduled departure of the train.

"You fellows remind me of the day they were going to hang the horse thief," Mr. Lincoln said. "The road to the hanging place was so crowded with people going to the execution that the wagon taking the prisoner was delayed. As more and more people crowded ahead the prisoner called out, 'What's your hurry, there ain't goin' to be any fun till I git there.' "

The day after his address at Gettysburg he wrote an answer to a letter of congratulation from Edward Everett, the most renowned orator, with whom he had shared the speakers' rostrum at the ceremonies.

"Your kind note of today is received. In our respective parts yesterday, you could not have been excused to make a short address, nor I a long one. I am pleased to know that, in your judgement, the little I did say was not entirely a failure."

"I remember going into Mr. Stanton's room in the War Department the day after the Gettysburg celebration," Charles A. Dana commented, "and he said: 'Have you seen these Gettysburg speeches?'

" 'No,' I said, 'I didn't know you had them.'

"He said, 'Yes, and the people will be delighted with them. Edward Everett has made a speech that will make many columns in the newspapers, and Mr. Lincoln's, perhaps forty or fifty lines. Everett's is the speech of a scholar, polished to the last possibility. It is elegant and it is learned; but Lincoln's speech will be read by a thousand men where one reads

Everett's, and will be remembered as long as anybody's speeches are remembered who speaks the English language.' "

[14]

The military news was beginning to be all Grant, and in March, 1864, the President commissioned him lieutenant general and placed him in command of all the Union Armies.

"Just after receiving my commission as lieutenant general," Grant wrote, "the President called me aside to speak to me privately. After a brief reference to the military situation, he said he thought he could illustrate what he wanted to say by a story, which he related as follows:

" 'At one time there was a great war among the animals, and one side had great difficulty in getting a commander who had sufficient confidence in himself. Finally they found a monkey by the name of Jocko, who said he thought he could command their army if his tail could be made a little longer. So they got more tail and spliced it onto his caudal appendage. He looked at it admiringly, and then thought he ought to have a little more still. This was added, and again he called for more. The splicing process was repeated many times, until they had coiled Jocko's tail around the room, filling all the space. Still he called for more tail, and, there being no other place to coil it, they began wrapping it around his shoulders. He continued his call for more, and they kept on winding the additional tail around him until its weight broke him down.'

"I saw the point, and, rising from my chair, replied:

" 'Mr. President, I will not call for more assistance unless I find it impossible to do with what I already have.' "

The new field commander then drove his armies toward

Richmond in one of the most brutal, bruising campaigns of the war.

The President went to Baltimore in April to deliver an address. He included some comments on the meaning of the word liberty:

"The world has never had a good definition of the word liberty, and the American people, just now, are much in want of one. We all declare for liberty; but in using the same *word* we do not all mean the same *thing*. With some the word liberty may mean for each man to do as he pleases with himself, and the product of his labor; while with others the same word may mean for some men to do as they please with other men, and the product of other men's labor. Here are two, not only different, but incompatable (*sic*) things, called by the same name—liberty. And it follows that each of the things is, by the respective parties, called by two different and incompatible names—liberty and tyranny.

"The shepherd drives the wolf from the sheep's throat, for which the sheep thanks the shepherd as a *liberator*, while the wolf denounces him for the same act as a destroyer of liberty, especially as the sheep was a black one. Plainly the sheep and the wolf are not agreed upon a definition of the word liberty; and precisely the same difference prevails today among us human creatures, even in the North, and all professing to love liberty. Hence we behold the processes by which thousands are daily passing from under the yoke of bondage, hailed by some as the advance of liberty, and bewailed by others as the destruction of all liberty."

About this time Billy Brown, the Springfield storekeeper, went to Washington to call upon the President. He told Ida Tarbell of his visit.

"That night I footed it up to the Soldiers' Home where Mr. Lincoln was living then, right among the sick soldiers in their tents. There was lots of people setting around in a little room, waiting for him, but there wasn't nobody there I knowed, and I was feeling a little funny, when a door opened

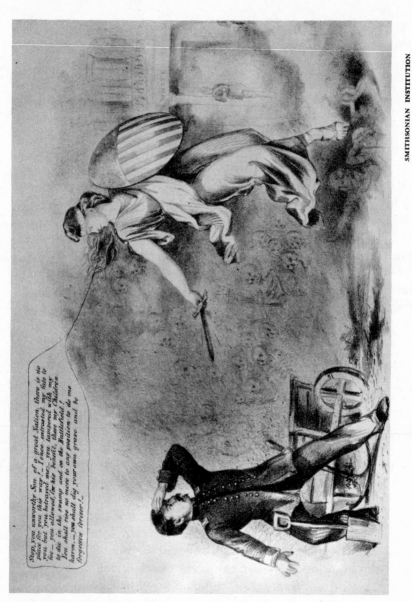

Columbia and an army of corpses halt the Democratic candidate on his way to the White House.

and out came little John Nicolay. He came down this way, so I just went up and says, 'How'd you do, John; where's Mr. Lincoln?'

"Well, John didn't seem over glad to see me.

"Have you an appointment with Mr. Lincoln?' he says.

" 'No, sir,' I says; 'I ain't , and it ain't necessary. Maybe it's all right and fitting for them as wants post offices to have appointments, but I reckon Mr. Lincoln's old friends don't need them, so you just trot along, Johnnie, and tell him Billy Brown's here, and see what he says.' Well, he kind of flushed up and set his lips together, but he knowed me, and so went off.

"In about two minutes the door popped open and out came Mr. Lincoln, his face all lit up. He saw me first thing and he laid hold of me, and just shook my hands fit to kill. 'Billy,' he says, 'now I am glad to see you. Come right in. You're going to stay to supper with Mary and me.'

"Didn't I know it? Think being President would change him? Not a mite. Well, he had a right smart lot of people to see, but as soon as he was through we went out on the back stoop and sat down and talked and talked. He asked me about pretty nigh everybody in Springfield. I just let loose and told him about the weddings and the births and funerals and the buildings, and I guess there wasn't a yarn I'd heard in the three and a half years he'd been away that I didn't spin for him. Laugh—you'd ought to hear him laugh—just did my heart good, for I could see what they'd been doing to him. Always was a thin man, but Lordy, he was thinner than ever now, and his face was kind of drawn and gray—enough to make you cry.

"Well, we had supper and then talked some more, and about ten o'clock I started downtown. Wanted me to stay all night, but I says to myself, 'Billy, don't you overdo it. You've cheered him up, and let him remember it when he's tired.' So I said, 'Nope, Mr. Lincoln, can't, going back to Springfield tomorrow. Ma don't like to have me away, and my boy ain't no great shakes at keeping store.'

" 'Billy,' he says, 'what did you come down here for?'

" 'I came to see you, Mr. Lincoln.'

" 'But you ain't asked me for anything, Billy. What is it? Out with it. Want a post office?' he said, giggling, for he knowed I didn't.

" 'No, Mr. Lincoln, just wanted to see you—felt kind of lonesome—been so long since I'd seen you, and I was afraid I'd forget some of them yarns if I didn't unload soon.'

"Well, sir, you ought to seen his face as he looked at me.

" 'Billy Brown,' he says, slow-like, 'do you mean to tell me you came all the way from Springfield, Illinois, just to have a visit with me; that you ain't got no complaints in your pockets, nor any advice up your sleeve?'

" 'Yes, sir,' I says, 'That's about it, and I'll be durned if I wouldn't go to Europe to see you, if I couldn't do it no other way, Mr. Lincoln.'

"Well, Sir, I was never so astonished in all my life. He just grabbed my hand and shook it nearly off, and the tears just poured down his face and he says:

" 'Billy, you'll never know just what good you've done me. I'm homesick, Billy, just plumb homesick, and it seems as if this war would never be over. Many a night I can see the boys dying on the fields and can hear their mothers crying for them at home, and I can't help it, Billy, I have to send them down there. We've got to save the Union, Billy, we've got to.' "

Propaganda for total victory. In this cartoon, which appeared before the 1864 election, artist Thomas Nast urged the North not to compromise.

[15]

On June 7, 1864, Lincoln was nominated for a second term. About the only way he could be defeated, he was told, would be if Grant took Richmond and decided to run for the Presidency against him.

"I feel," Mr. Lincoln replied, "very much like the man who said he didn't want to die particularly, but if he had got to die that was precisely the disease he would like to die of."

Late in June, while the Army of Northern Virginia was being painfully and slowly forced back upon Richmond and Sherman was advancing on Atlanta, Lincoln visited Grant at his headquarters in City Point, Virginia.

The two men visited the Dutch Gap canal project which aimed to cut through a loop in the James River and facilitate a new advance on Richmond.

"After taking him around and showing him all the points of interest," Grant wrote, "explaining how, in blowing up one portion of the work that was being excavated, the explosion had thrown the material back into, and had filled up, part of the work already completed, he turned to me and said:

"Grant, do you know what this reminds me of? Out in Springfield, Illinois, there was a blacksmith who didn't have much to do one day. He took a piece of soft iron that had been in his shop for some time, and for which he had no special use, and, starting up his fire, began to heat it. When he got it hot he carried it to the anvil and began to hammer it, rather thinking that he would weld it into an agricultural implement. He pounded away for some time until he got it fashioned into some shape, when he discovered that the iron would not hold out to complete the implement he had in mind. He then put it back into the forge, heated it up again, and recommenced hammering with an ill-defined notion that he would make a claw hammer, but after a time he came to the conclusion that there was more iron there than was needed to make a claw hammer. Again he heated it, and thought he would make an ax. After hammering it and welding it into shape, knocking off the oxidized iron, he concluded that there was not enough iron left to make an ax that would be any use. He was getting tired and a little disgusted at the result of his various essays. So he filled his forge full of coal, and, after placing the iron in the center of the heap, took the bellows and worked up a tremendous blast, bringing the iron to white heat. Then with his tongs he lifted it from the bed of coals, and, thrusting it into a tub of water near by, exclaimed with an oath, 'Well, if I can't make anything else out of you, I will make a fizzle, anyhow.'

"I replied that I was afraid that was about what I had done with the Dutch Gap Canal."

In August, the Democratic party met in Chicago to nominate a candidate to oppose Lincoln in the November election. The Democratic platform was simple: The armies would be ordered to cease hostilities and go home, and the Southern states would be invited to join a convention to restore the Union. After considerable pulling and hauling the Convention then concluded to nominate General George McClellan, who, having been dismissed as commander of the Union Armies by the President in 1862, was considered to be a most desirable candidate.

The ensuing campaign caused a good deal of political activity within the Army. Stanton was furious: this, to him, seemed damaging to the war effort. One officer, who had been mustered out of the service at Stanton's order, appealed to the President. Mr. Lincoln reinstated the officer, saying:

"If I should muster out all my generals who avow themselves Democrats, there would be a sad thinning out of commanding officers in the army. When the military duties of an officer are fully and faithfully performed, he can manage his politics in his own way; we've no more to do with them than with his religion. Supporting General McClellan for the Presidency is no violation of army regulations, and as a question of taste in choosing between him and me, well, I'm the longest, but he's better looking."

The victory of David G. Farragut at Mobile Bay in early August was followed by Sherman's entrance into Atlanta on September 2, and those who wanted Mr. Lincoln re-elected took heart.

Lincoln visited Sherman's army in Georgia, and the general reported an incident of the inspection trip.

" 'I saw an officer with whom I had had a little difficulty that morning. His face was pale and his lips compressed. I foresaw a scene, but sat on the front seat of the carriage as quiet as a lamb. The officer forced his way through the crowd to the carriage and said: 'Mr. President, I have a cause of grievance. This morning I went to speak to General Sherman, and he threatened to shoot me.' Mr. Lincoln said, 'Threatened to shoot you?' 'Yes, sir, threatened to shoot me.' Mr. Lincoln looked at him, then at me, and, stooping his long form towards the officer, said to him in a loud stage whisper, easily heard for yards around, 'Well, were I you, and he threatened to shoot me, I would not trust him, for I believe he would do it.' "

On November 8, Lincoln won a clear, but far from overwhelming victory. Had the close margins in Ohio, Pennsylvania, and New York not held for the President, McClellan might well have been elected.

During the last cold winter of the war the President worked harder than ever. A Union officer who called upon Mr. Lincoln with a plea for the life of one of his soldiers, whom he believed to have been unjustly condemned, reported that at the close of the interview he had remarked:

"I beg your pardon, Mr. Lincoln, but is it not a most exhausting thing to sit here hearing all these appeals, and have all of this business on your hands?"

"Yes, yes," the President replied, "no man ought to be ambitious to be President of the United States; and when this war is over, and it won't be very long—I tell my Tad that we will go back to the farm, where I was happier as a boy when I dug potatoes at twenty-five cents a day than I am now; I tell him I will buy him a mule and a pony, and he shall have a little cart and make a little garden in a field all his own. Yes, and I will be far happier than I have ever been here."

On the third of February, 1865, Mr. Lincoln and Mr. Seward went to Hampton Roads to meet with three representatives of the Confederacy, who wanted to discuss terms for ending the war. The three-man Southern delegation insisted that Jefferson Davis be recognized as the president of the Confederacy in negotiating with the United States Government, and cited the correspondence between Charles I and Parliament as a precedent for this negotiation between a constitutional ruler and rebels.

"Upon such questions of history," said Mr. Lincoln, "I must refer you to Mr. Seward, for he is posted on such things, and I don't profess to be; but my only distinct recollection of the matter is that Charles lost his head."

It had been reported that Lincoln brought out a sheet of blank paper at the conference table and showed it to the Vice President of the Confederacy, Alexander H. Stephens, saying "let me write UNION at the top of the page, and you may write below it anything you please." He went on to say that the rebel leaders had plainly forfeited all right to immunity from punishment for the highest crime known to the law.

Robert M. T. Hunter, a member of the Confederate delegation, listened soberly and said: "Then, Mr. President, if we understand you correctly, you think that we of the Confederacy have committed treason; we are traitors to your govern-

Lincoln won the election by a margin that was large but far from overwhelming. Cartoonist Frank Bellew showed him being carried by the majority, while McClellan, in the background, sank under the minority.

ment; that we have forfeited our rights, and are proper subjects for the hangman. Is not that about what your words imply?"

"Yes," said Mr. Lincoln, "you have stated the proposition better than I did. That is about the size of it."

There was a pause, after which Mr. Hunter replied: "Well, Mr. Lincoln, we have about concluded that we shall not be hanged as long as you are President—if we behave ourselves."

In discussing the President's insistence that the Emancipation Proclamation be accepted, Mr. Hunter observed that the slaves, having been used to working under compulsion for so long, would, if suddenly freed, precipitate the whole society of the South into chaos. No work would be done, and the whites and blacks would starve together.

The President replied: "Mr. Hunter, you ought to know a good deal more about the matter than I, for you have always lived under the slave system. I can only say in answer to your statement of the case that it reminds me of the story of a man out in Illinois, who undertook a few years ago to raise a very large herd of hogs. It was a great trouble to feed them; and how to get around this was a puzzle to him. At length he hit upon the plan of planting an immense field to potatoes, and when they were sufficiently grown, he turned the whole herd into the field and let them have full swing, thus saving not only the labor of feeding the hogs, but also that of digging the potatoes. Charmed by his sagacity, he stood one day by the fence counting his hogs when a neighbor came along.

" 'Well, well,' he said, 'this is all very fine. Your hogs are doing very well just now; but you know out here the frost comes early, and the ground freezes a foot deep. Then what are they going to do?'

"This was a view of the matter that the farmer had not taken into account. Butchering time for hogs was away on in December or January. He scratched his head and at length said, 'Well, it may come pretty hard on their snouts, but I don't see but it will be root hog, or die.' "

The President also required the immediate cessation of hostilities and the disbanding of the Confederate forces. The terms were unacceptable, and the conference produced no settlement.

Henry J. Raymond, founder and editor of *The New York Times,* wrote that the President on at least one occasion opened a very serious conference with several senators by reading aloud a recent Petroleum V. Nasby column and saying:

"I am going to write Petroleum to come down here, and I intend to tell him, if he will communicate his talent to me, I will swap places with him."

Raymond quoted a critic on William Shakespeare: "The spirit which held the woe of *Lear* and the tragedy of *Hamlet* would have broken if it had not also had the humor of *The Merry Wives of Windsor* and the merriment of *A Midsummer Night's Dream.*"

"This is as true of Mr. Lincoln as it was of William Shakespeare," Raymond concluded; "the capacity to tell and enjoy a good anecdote undoubtedly lengthened his life."

By a coincidence, two sons of Robert E. Lee were taken prisoner. They were held at Fortress Monroe where they were to be executed in reprisal for the impending hanging of two Union officers.

Lee hastened to Richmond to request Jefferson Davis to intercede on behalf of his boys.

"You need not worry," Davis said, "because Abraham Lincoln will not permit such an outrage."

"Stanton will carry out his diabolical purpose," Lee replied, "and Lincoln will know nothing of it until it has been accomplished and both my sons are dead."

Davis prepared a telegram for the President of the United States, had it carried through the battle lines and duly delivered to the White House. Lincoln read it and immediately

Jefferson Davis's nightmare. Lincoln had been elected for another term.

summoned the Secretary of War. Stanton stated the case earnestly, and concluded by saying:

" 'Mr. President, the lives of those two Union captains are as precious to their families as are the lives of those Lee boys to their family. If our men are hanged at Richmond, both the sons of Robert E. Lee should be hanged."

"Stanton," said the President, "if a crime is committed in Richmond I cannot prevent it, but a crime like that under my jurisdiction would stamp upon my heart, by command of my conscience, the word 'murderer.' Stanton, it can't be done . . . it can't be done . . . we are not savages."

Lincoln picked up a Bible from his desk and said: "Let us see what the Book says. Here is a command from Almighty God in His Book. Read these words yourself: 'Vengeance is mine; I will repay, saith the Lord.' "

The President wrote a message, signed it, and directed that it be dispatched forthwith to Fortress Monroe:

"Immediately release both the sons of Robert E. Lee and send them back to their father."

The appeals for pardons were endless. A Southern woman who had come to see Lincoln on behalf of her husband, who was confined in a Northern prison, mentioned that the prisoner was a very religious man.

"I'm glad to hear that," Mr. Lincoln said, "because any man who wants to disrupt this Union needs all the religion in sight to save him."

[16]

March 4, 1865, dawned cold, wet, and windy, but about the time Mr. Lincoln read the last paragraph of his carefully prepared second inaugural, the sun burst forth. There were many who heard the words he spoke who thought they had listened to a prayer rather than a speech.

" 'I saw him on his return, at three o'clock, after the performance was over," Walt Whitman wrote. "He was in his plain two-horse barouche, and looked very much worn and tired; the lines indeed, of vast responsibilities, intricate questions, and demands of life and death, cut deeper than ever upon his dark brown face; yet all the old goodness, tenderness, sadness, and canny shrewdness underneath the furrows. (I never see that man without feeling that he is one to be attached to, for his combination of purest, heartiest, tenderness, and native Western form of manliness.) By his side sat his little boy of ten years. There were no soldiers, only a lot of civilians on horseback, with huge yellow scarfs over their shoulders, riding around the carriage. (At the inauguration four years ago, he rode down and back again surrounded by a dense mass of armed cavalrymen, eight deep, with drawn sabers; and there were sharp-shooters stationed at every corner of the route.)"

On April 2 General Lee notified Jefferson Davis that Richmond was no longer defensible by his army, and the president and cabinet members of the Confederacy evacuated the city. While the North celebrated the capture of the Confederate capital, Grant began the swift harassment and encirclement of Lee's army. Knowing that the end was near, the President wanted to avoid an annihilating confrontation. Seven days later, Lee's army, starving and spent, found itself almost completely surrounded. On Palm Sunday, 1865, General Lee surrendered.

All the following day the people of Washington milled around the White House, shouting for Lincoln and Stanton. The President had started work on a speech that he planned to make on the eleventh, but he could not withhold himself completely from the rejoicing.

He addressed one group as follows: "Fellow Citizens: I am very greatly rejoiced to find that an occasion has occurred so

One Union or two? In February, 1865, a Confederate delegation, headed by Alexander H. Stephens, met with the President to discuss ending the war. But neither side was willing to accept the other's demands, and the conference failed.

pleasurable that the people cannot restrain themselves. (Cheers.) I suppose that arrangements are being made for some sort of a formal demonstration, this, or perhaps, to-morrow night. (Cries of 'We can't wait,' 'We want it now,' etc.) If there should be such a demonstration, I, of course, will be called upon to respond, and I shall have nothing to say if you dribble it all out of me before. (Laughter and applause.) I see you have a band of music with you. (Voices, 'We have two or three.') I propose closing up this interview by the band performing a particular tune which I will name. Before this is done, however, I wish to mention one or two little circumstances connected with it. I have always thought 'Dixie' one of the best tunes I have ever heard. Our adversaries over the way attempted to appropriate it, but I insisted yesterday that we fairly captured it. (Applause.) I presented the question to the Attorney General, and he gave it as his legal opinion that it is our lawful prize. (Laughter and applause.) I now request the band to favor me with its performance."

The bands played "Dixie" and "Yankee Doodle," the President called for cheers for General Grant and the Army, then for the Navy; when he turned away from the window, there was a great cheer for him.

The President's old friend Joshua Speed was at the White House for a visit, and the next morning watched while the President granted a request for the release of several draft resisters whose case was presented by two ladies. When Speed and Lincoln were alone, the President said:

"That old lady was no counterfeit. The mother spoke out in all the features of her face. It is more than one can often say that in doing right one has made two people happy in one day. Speed, die when I may, I want it said of me by those who know me best, that I always plucked a thistle and planted a flower where I thought a flower would grow."

Later that day Speed was invited to an informal Cabinet

meeting to discuss the disposition of Jefferson Davis and other Confederate leaders. Each member of the Cabinet gave his opinion. Hanging the traitors was the most widely held verdict.

Speed said: "I have had the opinion of your ministers, Mr. Lincoln, now I would like to hear yours."

"Well, Josh," replied the President, "when I was a boy in Indiana, I went to a neighbor's house one morning and found a boy of my own size holding a coon by a string. I asked him what he had and what he was doing.

"He says, 'It's a coon. Dad cotched six last night, and killed all but this poor little cuss. Dad told me to hold him until he came back, and I'm afraid he's going to kill this one too; and oh, Abe, I do wish he'd get away.'

" 'Well, why don't you let him loose?'

" 'That wouldn't be right; and if I let him go, Dad would give me hell. But if he got away by himself, it would be all right.'

"Now," said the President, "if Jeff Davis and those other fellows will only get away, it will be all right. But if we should catch them, and I should let them go, 'Dad would give me hell.' "

In a similar vein, when the Assistant Secretary of War notified the President that the provost marshal of Portland, Maine, had reported that the well-known Confederate agent Jacob Thompson was about to flee his city for parts unknown, Mr. Lincoln replied:

"Let me tell you a story. There was an Irish soldier here last summer who wanted something to drink stronger than water, and stopped at a drug-shop where he espied a soda fountain. 'Mr. Doctor,' said he, 'give me, please, a glass of soda-water, an' if yez can put in a few drops of whiskey, unbeknownst to anyone, I'll be obliged.'

"Now," continued Mr. Lincoln, "if Jake Thompson is permitted to go through Maine 'unbeknownst to anyone,' what's the harm?"

The lines of humor and responsibility were sharply etched in the War President's face. After the war was over, he faced the new task of binding up the Nation's wounds. This pen-and-ink drawing appeared in *Harper's Weekly* on the day of his death—April 15, 1865.

The kind words the President had to say for the enemy brought him rebukes from some of his friends. One lady said she wondered how he could speak kindly of his enemies, when he should rather destroy them.

"But, Madam," replied the President, "do I not destroy them when I make them my friends?"

The days of Holy Week passed quickly. The President worked long hours, but his friends noticed a new air of freshness and relaxation about him. Good Friday morning there was a Cabinet meeting, which had hoped for news from General Sherman.

"The President remarked it would, he had no doubt, come soon," Gideon Welles recorded in his diary; "for he had, last night, the usual dream which he had preceding nearly every great and important event of the war. Generally, the news had been favorable which succeeded the dream, and the dream itself was always the same. I inquired what this remarkable dream could be. He said it related to my element, the water; that he seemed to be in some singular, and indescribable vessel, and that he was moving with great rapidity towards an indefinite shore."

After the Cabinet meeting Ward H. Lamon, marshal of the District of Columbia, came to the President with a request for a pardon.

"Lamon," said the President, "have you ever heard how the Patagonians eat oysters? They open them and throw the shells out of the window until the pile gets higher than the house, and then they move. I feel today like starting a new pile of pardons, and I may as well begin just here."

In the afternoon Mr. Lincoln went for a long carriage ride with his wife. In the evening he went to the theater.

[17]

Billy Brown was home in Springfield. "I tell you," he said,
"it was a great day out here when we heard Lee had surrendered. 'Twas just like getting converted to have the war
over. Somehow, the only thing I could think of was how glad
Mr. Lincoln would be. Me and Ma reckoned he'd come right
out and make us a visit and get rested, and we began right off
to make plans about the reception we'd give him—brass
bands—parade—speeches—fireworks—everything. Seems as if
I couldn't think about anything else. I was coming down to
open the store one morning, and all the way down I was
planning how I'd decorate the windows and how I'd tie a flag
on that old chair, when I see Hiram Jones coming toward me.
He looked so old and all bent over I didn't know what had
happened. 'Hiram,' I said, 'What's the matter? Be you sick?'

"'Billy,' he says, and he couldn't hardly say it, 'Billy,
they've killed Mr. Lincoln.'

"Well, I just turned cold all over, and then I flared up.
'Hiram Jones,' I says, 'you're lying, you're crazy. How dare
you tell me that? It ain't so.'

"'Don't, Billy,' he says, 'don't go on so. I ain't lying. It's so.
He'll never come back, Billy. He's dead.' And he fell to sob-
bing out loud, right there in the street, and somehow I knew
it was true."

Abraham Lincoln—A Chronology

Abraham Lincoln—A Chronology

1809

Feb. 12.
Abraham Lincoln born in Hardin County, Kentucky, three miles south of present-day Hodgenville.

1816

Autumn.
Thomas Lincoln and family move to what is now Spencer County, Indiana.

1818

Oct. 5.
Abraham's mother, Nancy Hanks Lincoln, dies of milk sickness.

1819

Dec. 2.
Abraham's father, Thomas Lincoln, and Mrs. Sarah Bush Johnston are married in Elizabethtown, Kentucky.

1828

Autumn.
Lincoln makes his first trip by flatboat to New Orleans.

1830

Mar. 1.
Thomas Lincoln's family moves to Illinois.

Mar. 15.
The Lincoln party arrives at Decatur, Illinois, and establishes a new home eight miles southwest of town on the Sangamon River. After the winter of 1830–1831 Thomas Lincoln and family move to Coles County, Illinois. The last of their four homes in that county is now Lincoln Log Cabin State Park.

Apr.–July.	Lincoln pilots the flatboat with produce of Denton Offut to New Orleans and returns to New Salem, eighteen miles northwest of Springfield.
Aug. 1.	Lincoln casts his first vote and gains a reputation as a story-teller; and a month later becomes a store clerk.

1832

Mar. 9.	Lincoln announces his candidacy for the legislature.
Apr. 7.	Lincoln is elected a captain in the 31st Regiment Illinois Militia.
Apr. 21.	Lincoln is elected captain of a volunteer company enlisted to drive Black Hawk and his band west of the Mississippi River.
July 10.	Lincoln writes the mustering out roll for Captain Early. It is certified by Lieutenant Robert Anderson, who commanded at Fort Sumter in 1861.
Aug. 6.	Lincoln is defeated for the legislature. He runs eighth in a field of thirteen candidates.

1833

Jan. 15.	William F. Berry and Lincoln purchase the New Salem store formerly owned by Reuben Radford.
May 7.	Lincoln is appointed postmaster of New Salem by President Jackson. He serves until the post office is moved to Petersburg on May 30, 1836.

1834

Jan. 6.	Lincoln's first survey, as a deputy surveyor of Sangamon County, is of 800 acres for Reason Shipley.
Aug. 4.	Lincoln is elected one of four Sangamon County members of the lower house of the Illinois General Assembly. He is re-elected in 1836, 1838, and 1840.

Sept. 30.	Lincoln makes his first town survey, New Boston on the Mississippi. In 1836 he surveys Petersburg, Huron, Albany, and Bath.
Dec. 1.	Lincoln takes his seat in the lower house of the Ninth General Assembly at Vandalia.

1835

Aug. 25.	Ann Rutledge dies at farm home seven miles northwest of New Salem.

1837

Apr. 15.	Lincoln, admitted to the bar March 1, becomes the law partner of John T. Stuart in the firm of Stuart & Lincoln.

1838

Dec. 3.	Lincoln is beaten for speaker of the House at the opening of the Eleventh General Assembly.

1839

June 24.	Lincoln begins a term as trustee of the town of Springfield. He serves until the new city charter goes into effect in April, 1840.
July 4.	Illinois state government is moved from Vandalia to Springfield.
Sept. 23.	Lincoln begins practice on the newly organized Eighth Judicial Circuit. He continues to attend these courts until his nomination for the presidency.
Oct. 8.	Lincoln is chosen one of the presidential electors by the Whig convention.
Dec. 3.	Lincoln is admitted to practice in the United States Circuit Court by Judge Nathaniel Pope.

1841

April 14.	The partnership of Stuart & Lincoln is dissolved and Lincoln becomes the junior partner of Stephen T. Logan.
Nov. 4.	Lincoln and Mary Todd are married at the

home of her brother-in-law, Ninian W. Edwards, by the Rev. Charles Dresser, minister of the Episcopal Church.

1843

Aug. 1.
Robert Todd Lincoln, first child of the Lincolns, is born at the Globe Tavern, where they are then residing.

1844

May 2.
The Lincolns move into the house at Eighth and Jackson streets, their home until they go to the White House.

Oct. 30.
Lincoln speaks at Rockport, Indiana, near his boyhood home, at the close of his campaign tour of southern Illinois, Kentucky and Indiana, for Henry Clay.

Dec. 9.
William H. Herndon is admitted to the bar. The firm of Lincoln & Herndon is organized soon afterward.

1846

Mar. 10.
Edward Baker Lincoln, second child of the Lincolns, is born and named for Edward Dickinson Baker, a friend and political associate.

Aug. 3.
Lincoln is the only Whig elected among seven congressmen in Illinois. His majority of 1,511 votes over the Rev. Peter Cartwright is unprecedented.

1847

Dec. 6.
Lincoln takes his seat in the Thirtieth Congress.

Dec. 22.
Lincoln presents a series of resolutions requesting President Polk to inform the House whether the "spot" where American blood was first shed in the Mexican War was not within territory claimed by Mexico.

1848

June 7–9.   Lincoln attends national Whig convention, at Philadelphia. General Zachary Taylor nominated for president.

1849

June 21.   Lincoln fails to get the appointment as commissioner of the General Land Office, for which he has made a special trip to Washington.

Aug. 21.   Lincoln declines appointment as secretary of Oregon Territory.

Sept. 27.   Lincoln declines appointment as governor of Oregon Territory.

1850

Feb. 1.   Edward Baker Lincoln dies.

Dec. 21.   William Wallace Lincoln, third son of the Lincolns, is born.

1851

Jan. 17.   Lincoln's father, Thomas, born in Virginia in 1778, dies in Coles County, Illinois.

1853

Apr. 4.   Thomas (Tad) Lincoln, fourth son of the Lincolns, is born.

1854

May 30.   The Kansas-Nebraska Act is signed.

Oct. 16.   Lincoln delivers at Peoria a speech on "the repeal of the Missouri Compromise, and the propriety of its restoration."

Nov. 7.   Lincoln is elected to the Illinois legislature. He declines the office on November 27 to become a candidate for the U.S. Senate.

1855

Feb. 8.   Lincoln defeated for the U.S. Senate. To forestall election by the General Assembly of Joel A. Matteson he throws his votes to Lyman Trumbull.

1856

May 29. Lincoln delivers his famous "Lost Speech" at the organization of the Republican Party at Bloomington, Illinois.

June 19. Lincoln receives 110 votes on the informal ballot for vice-president at the first Republican National Convention at Philadelphia.

1857

June 26. Lincoln delivers in Springfield his first major speech against the Dred Scott decision.

Aug. 12. Lincoln receives his largest legal fee, $5,000, for winning Illinois Central Railroad v. County of McLean in the state Supreme Court.

1858

June 16. "Abraham Lincoln is the first and only choice of the Republicans of Illinois for the United States Senate." Lincoln accepts the nomination and delivers the famous "House Divided" speech in the Hall of the House of Representatives of the statehouse (present Sangamon County Courthouse).

Aug. 21. The first Lincoln-Douglas debate is held at Ottawa. Subsequent debates are held at Freeport (Aug. 27), Jonesboro (Sept. 15), Charleston (Sept. 18), Galesburg (Oct. 7), Quincy (Oct. 13) and Alton (Oct. 15).

Nov. 2. Lincoln gets a majority of the votes, but the gerrymandered legislative districts give Douglas his re-election to the U.S. Senate.

1859

Sept. 16–17. Lincoln speaks twice in Columbus, Ohio, and in Dayton, Hamilton and Cincinnati.

Sept. 30. Lincoln addresses the Wisconsin State Fair at

Milwaukee. He makes a political speech there in the evening, and in Beloit and Janesville the day following.

Dec. 1–3.   Lincoln speaks in Kansas, at Elwood, Troy, Doniphan, Atchison and Leavenworth a few days before the territorial election.

Dec. 20.   Lincoln sends his autobiography to Jesse W. Fell. "If any thing be made out of it, I wish it to be modest."

1860

Feb. 27.   Lincoln delivers his Cooper Union Address in New York City, which is printed in full by the *New York Tribune*.

Feb. 28.   Lincoln begins a two-week speaking tour of New England.

May 18.   Lincoln is nominated for President of the United States on the third ballot at the Republican National Convention in Chicago. Hannibal Hamlin of Maine is nominated for Vice-President.

July.   Robert Lincoln enrolls in Harvard University. Graduating in 1864, he becomes a captain on General Ulysses S. Grant's staff.

Oct. 19.   Lincoln replies to a letter from eleven-year-old Grace Bedell of Westfield, New York: "As to the whiskers, having never worn any, do you not think people would call it a piece of silly affection if I were to begin it now?" But he soon became the first bearded President.

Nov. 6.   Lincoln is the first Republican President of the United States, defeating Douglas (Northern Democrat), John C. Breckinridge (Southern Democrat), and John Bell (Constitutional Unionist).

Dec. 20.   South Carolina is the first state to secede.

1861

Feb. 4.   Representatives of South Carolina, Georgia,

Florida, Alabama, Mississippi, and Louisiana meet in Montgomery, Alabama, to form the Confederate States of America. Texas, which had also seceded, is not represented. Jefferson Davis is elected President and Alexander H. Stephens Vice-President.

Feb. 11. Lincoln delivers his "Farewell Address" to the people of Springfield at the Great Western Railroad station.

Feb. 23. Lincoln arrives in Washington after a twelve-day trip and many public appearances and speeches.

Mar. 4. Lincoln is inaugurated the sixteenth President of the United States.

Apr. 12–14. Fort Sumter is attacked, and after thirty-four hours of bombardment, surrenders to the Confederate forces.

Apr. 15. Lincoln convenes an extra session of Congress to meet on July 4, and calls for 75,000 volunteers. As a result Virginia, North Carolina, Tennessee and Arkansas secede. The Confederate capital is moved to Richmond, Virginia.

Apr. 19, 27. Lincoln proclaims a blockade of the Confederate states from Virginia to Texas.

May 3. By proclamation Lincoln calls for 42,034 three-year volunteers, 22,714 additional men for the regular Army and 18,000 for the Navy.

May 24. Northern troops take over Alexandria and the Virginia heights, and begin the string of forts to protect Washington.

June 3. Stephen A. Douglas dies in Chicago at the age of forty-eight. His stirring address in Springfield, April 25, had united Illinois and encouraged thousands to enter the Union Army.

July 21. General Irvin McDowell's army defeated at Bull Run.

July 22. Congress votes $500,000,000 to support the war, and gives Lincoln war powers.

July 27.	Lincoln brings General George B. McClellan to Washington to command all the forces there and the Army of the Potomac.
Nov. 1.	General Winfield Scott's resignation is accepted and McClellan is made general-in-chief.
Nov. 8.	Mason and Slidell, Confederate commissioners to Great Britain and France, are seized on the British steamer *Trent*.
Dec. 10.	Congress resolves on the appointment of a joint committee to inquire into the conduct of the war.
Dec. 28.	The surrender of Mason and Slidell to the British authorities is ordered by the government.

1862

Jan. 13.	Lincoln sends Simon Cameron as minister to Russia, and replaces him with Edwin M. Stanton as Secretary of War.
Feb. 6, 16.	Fort Henry on the Tennessee River and Fort Donelson on the Cumberland are taken by forces under General Grant, the first important victories of Northern armies.
Feb. 20.	William Wallace Lincoln, eleven-year-old son of the President, dies.
Mar. 8–9.	The Confederate ironclad *Merrimac* destroys the Northern ships in Hampton Roads, but Union ironclad *Monitor* forces it to retire.
Apr. 2.	McClellan arrives at Fortress Monroe to begin a four-month campaign on the Virginia Peninsula.
Apr. 6–7.	The Confederate attack at Pittsburg Landing or Shiloh, Tennessee, is repulsed with serious losses by both armies.
Apr. 25.	New Orleans is captured by Northern naval expedition under Admiral David G. Farragut.
May 15.	Lincoln approves the act establishing the Department of Agriculture.
May 20.	Lincoln signs the Homestead Law, which grants

	a quarter section of unoccupied land to home-steaders on payment of nominal fees after five years of actual residence.
June 20.	Slavery is prohibited in the territories by act of Congress.
July 1.	Lincoln approves the Union Pacific Railroad Company charter.
July 2.	The Morrill Agricultural College Land Grant Act becomes a law.
July 11.	Lincoln appoints Henry W. Halleck general-in-chief.
July 17.	Congress authorizes a draft of state militia, and empowers the President to accept Negroes for military and naval service.
Aug. 22.	In reply to criticism of administration policy by Horace Greeley, Lincoln writes: "My paramount object in this struggle *is* to save the Union, and is *not* either to save or to destroy slavery."
Aug. 30.	Northern forces under General John Pope are defeated at Bull Run.
Sept. 2.	Lincoln removes Pope and places McClellan in command of all troops around Washington.
Sept. 17.	McClellan stops General Robert E. Lee's Northern invasion in the Battle of Antietam, or Sharpsburg, Maryland.
Sept. 22.	President Lincoln issues preliminary proclamation of emancipation of slaves of rebels, to take effect January 1, 1863.
Sept. 24.	Lincoln suspends the writ of habeas corpus for all persons arrested by military authority.
Oct. 1–4.	Lincoln visits McClellan's army and the battlefield of Antietam.
Dec. 13.	The Army of the Potomac under command of General Ambrose E. Burnside is defeated at Fredericksburg, Virginia.
Dec. 31.	Lincoln approves the bill admitting West Virginia to the Union.

Jan. 1.   Lincoln issues the Emancipation Proclamation whereby slaves in areas held by Confederates are declared free.

Feb. 25.   Congress establishes a national currency; the National Bank Act is passed.

Mar. 3.   Lincoln approves the first draft law in the nation's history.

May 2–4.   The army under Hooker is defeated at Chancellorsville, Virginia.

July 1–3.   The Confederate invasion of Pennsylvania under Lee is defeated by General George G. Meade at Gettysburg.

July 4.   The long siege of Vicksburg by Grant results in the surrender of the Confederates under General John C. Pemberton.

Nov. 19.   Lincoln delivers his dedicatory address at the Gettysburg Cemetery.

Nov. 26.   The first national observance of Thanksgiving is held, as proclaimed by the President Oct. 3.

Dec. 8.   Lincoln issues a proclamation of amnesty to Confederates who take the oath of allegiance.

1864

Mar. 10.   The President appoints Ulysses S. Grant, who had become a lieutenant general on March 2, commander-in-chief of the armies.

May 5–12.   Grant and Lee are in constant battle in the Virginia Wilderness.

June 7.   The National Union Convention at Baltimore renominates Lincoln for President; Andrew Johnson of Tennessee is nominated for Vice-President.

June 20–24.   Lincoln visits Grant's army in Virginia.

June 28.   Congress repeals the Fugitive Slave Law.

Sept. 2.   General William T. Sherman takes Atlanta, a Northern victory which, with that of Farragut

	at Mobile Bay on August 5, insures Lincoln's re-election.
Nov. 8.	Lincoln is re-elected President over McClellan, the Democratic candidate.
Dec. 10.	Sherman's march "from Atlanta to the sea" concludes at Savannah, Georgia.

1865

Feb. 1.	Lincoln approves the Thirteenth Amendment, abolishing slavery.
Feb. 3.	Lincoln confers with representatives of the Confederacy on board the *River Queen* in Hampton Roads, Virginia.
Mar. 3.	The Freedman's Bureau is established by Congress to care for the Negroes.
Mar. 4.	Lincoln delivers his Second Inaugural Address.
Apr. 9.	Lee surrenders to Grant at Appomattox Court House, Virginia.
Apr. 11.	Lincoln delivers his last speech, from a window of the White House, in response to a serenade
Apr. 14.	Lincoln is shot at Ford's Theatre by the actor John Wilkes Booth.
Apr. 15.	Abraham Lincoln dies at 7:22 A.M.
Apr. 19.	Funeral services for President Lincoln are held in the White House.
Apr. 21–May 3.	The funeral train bears the remains of Lincoln on the journey to Springfield, Illinois.
May 4.	Lincoln is buried in Oak Ridge Cemetery on the north edge of Springfield. He leaves a net estate of $110,296.80, exclusive of real estate, to his widow and two surviving children. Lincoln's body is moved from the public receiving vault on December 21, 1865, to the temporary vault, and on September 19, 1871, to a crypt in the partially completed monument.
July 14, 1870.	Congress grants Mrs. Lincoln an annual pension of $3,000. On January 16, 1882, it is increased to $5,000, plus a gift of $15,000.

July 15, 1871.	"Tad" Lincoln dies of dropsy of the chest, in Chicago. He is buried in the Lincoln Tomb in Springfield.
Oct. 15, 1874.	The National Lincoln Monument Association, organized May 11, 1865, dedicates the partially completed Lincoln Tomb designed by Larkin G. Mead, Jr. President Ulysses S. Grant speaks briefly; Ex-Governor Richard J. Oglesby gives the principal address.
July 16, 1882.	Mrs. Lincoln dies in the Springfield home of her sister, Mrs. Ninian W. Edwards, where Lincoln courted and married her. She is buried in the Lincoln Tomb with her husband and three of their four sons.
June 16, 1887.	Robert Todd Lincoln and his wife Mary Harlan Lincoln present the Lincoln home in Springfield to the State of Illinois. The first floor has since been open to the public, visited by more than a third of a million people annually. The second floor was restored and opened to the public Feb. 12, 1955.
July 26, 1926.	Robert Lincoln dies and is buried in Arlington National Cemetery. Five years earlier he had left 18,350 items of his father's papers on deposit in the Library of Congress, not to be open to the public for twenty-one years after his death (July 26, 1947).
June 17, 1931.	The remodeled Lincoln Tomb is rededicated by President Herbert Hoover. It had been previously rebuilt in 1900–1901.

Selected Bibliography

Basler, Roy P., ed.: *The Collected Works of Abraham Lincoln*
Gross, Anthony: *Lincoln's Own Stories*
Hertz, Emanuel: *Lincoln Talks*
Jay, Allen: *Autobiography*
McClure, A. K.: *Lincoln's Own Yarns and Stories*
Nicolay, Helen: *Personal Traits of Abraham Lincoln*
Nicolay, John G. and Hay, John: *Abraham Lincoln: A History*
Rice, Allen Thorndike: *Reminiscences of Abraham Lincoln*
Sandburg, Carl: *Abraham Lincoln, The Prairie Years* and *Abraham Lincoln, The War Years*
Tarbell, Ida M.: *Life of Abraham Lincoln*
Tarbell, Ida M.: *He Knew Lincoln and Other Billy Brown Stories*
Welles, Gideon: *Diary of Gideon Welles*
Whipple, Wayne: *The Story Life of Lincoln*

Index

Index

Offutt's store, 10
"Old Tippecanoe," *see* Harrison, William H.

Pilgrim's Progress, The, 3
Polk, James K., 43
Pomeroy, Billy, case of, 118–119

Republican convention, first national, 49
Republican Party (*see also* election campaigns), 62, 64, 65
Rutledge, Ann, 19–20
Rutledge, James, 15, 19

Sangamo Journal:
  letters of "Rebecca," publication of, 31–32
  Lincoln's letter to, 20–21
Sangamon River, 11
Scott, Dred, 50–52
Scripps, John L., 47
Seward, William H., 10, 62–65, 76–77, 81, 95, 131
Sherman, William T., 119–121, 128, 130
Shields, James, 31–32
slavery, 10, 44–45, 50–52, 53–58, 66, 106–107
Slidell, John, 87
Southern States (*see also* Confederate States of America), secession of, 69, 72, 73
Speed, Joshua, 31, 139–140
Springfield courtroom, 21–23
"squatter" sovereignty, *see* Kansas-Nebraska Act

Stanton, Edwin M., 47, 81–82, 90–91, 99–102, 108, 114, 129, 134, 136
  on battle of Bull Run, 86
  on Lincoln, 81–82
  as Secretary of War, 90 *ff.*
Stephens, Alexander H., 131
Stevens, Thaddeus, 88, 111–112
Stuart, John T., 21
Sumner, Charles, 87
Sunderland, Byron, Rev., 104–107

Tarbell, Ida M., 40, 123
Thomas, George H., 119
Tibbles, Thomas H., 56–57
Todd, Elizabeth, 28
Todd, Mary, *see* Lincoln, Mary Todd
Trumbull, Lyman, 54
Try-weekly Steamer, 11

Union (*see also* Civil War), 77
  victory of, 137

Ward, Artemus, 99–100
Ward, Marcus, 99
Washington, D.C., 72–73, 83
Weed, Thurlow, 62, 81
Weems's *Life of Washington,* 7
Weik, Jesse, 36
Whig Party, 19
White, Hugh L., 21
Whitman, Walt, 137
Whitney, Henry, 49
"Wide-Awakes," 65
Wilson, Robert L., 19
Wilson, William B., 83–84